TALES OF
DARKNESS AND LIGHT

Tales of Darkness and Light

Soso Tham's *The Old Days of the Khasis*

Translated by Janet Hujon

https://www.openbookpublishers.com

Translation and Notes to the Text © 2018 Janet Hujon. Preface © 2018 Mark Turin.

World Oral Literature Series, vol. 9 | ISSN: 2050-7933 (Print); 2054-362X (Online)

ISBN Paperback: 978-1-78374-468-8
ISBN Hardback: 978-1-78374-469-5
ISBN Digital (PDF): 978-1-78374-470-1
ISBN Digital ebook (epub): 978-1-78374-471-8
ISBN Digital ebook (mobi): 978-1-78374-472-5
DOI: 10.11647/OBP.0137

Cover image: Barapani, Shillong (2009). Photo by Karthik Inbasekar. Flickr, https://www.flickr.com/photos/ikarthik/4438288322, CC BY-SA 2.0. Cover design: Anna Gatti.

All paper used by Open Book Publishers is SFI (Sustainable Forestry Initiative), PEFC (Programme for the Endorsement of Forest Certification Schemes) and Forest Stewardship Council(r)(FSC(r) certified.

Printed in the United Kingdom, United States, and Australia
by Lightning Source for Open Book Publishers (Cambridge, UK)

For Ma Wat, Papa and my children

Contents

Preface

Mark Turin

The World Oral Literature Series was established to serve two primary goals. First, by publishing in a range of innovative digital platforms, the series would challenge and change the shape, format and reach of academic publishing to connect important scholarship with a distributed global readership. Launched in 2012 with a new edition of Ruth Finnegan's discipline-defining *Oral Literature in Africa*, and celebrating its ninth volume with this publication, the breadth and quality of the scholarship in this series has made the study of Indigenous oral literature and oral traditions more visible. Second, a consequence of the approach to knowledge distribution taken by the World Oral Literature Series and our partners at Open Book is the amplification of innovative and collaborative publishing partnerships involving Indigenous intellectuals that more traditional academic imprints have been less able to support. Janet Hujon's beautiful translation of Soso Tham's *The Old Days of the Khasis*—so fittingly entitled *Tales of Darkness and Light*—realizes both of our goals with a gentle grace and formidable literary power.

Dr. Hujon is a writer and member of the Khasi community, an Indigenous and notably matrilineal ethnic group who have long inhabited what are now the states of Meghalaya and Assam in north-eastern India. Born in Shillong, Meghalaya, Hujon first took a Master's Degree in English Literature from the North Eastern Hill University and

    https://doi.org/10.11647/OBP.0137.14

then a Ph.D. in English Literature from the University of London. A versatile writer and original poet, Dr. Hujon's work has appeared in publications across Asia, North America and Europe. A self-identified inhabitant of two distinct if intersecting cultures—England and her original Khasi homeland—Janet Hujon is superbly well positioned to have taken on this ambitious project: conveying the subtlety of Soso Tham's timeless poetry to a global audience in English.

Described by Khasi writer and translator Kynpham Singh Nongkynrih as the "uncrowned, though acknowledged, poet laureate of the Khasis" in 2006, Soso Tham demonstrated his literary acumen and versatility through an important body of work that is narrated, sung and spoken by Khasis to this day, almost 80 years after his death. Janet Hujon captures the spirit of Soso Tham's writing in ways that are effortless and contemporary. For example, Soso Tham's reflection on the natural environment that has nurtured and protected his ancestors could be read as a prescient statement on declining ecological diversity and the dangers of climate change:

> Our hills were our guardians in the past
> Who will keep us from harm in days to come?

With characteristic restraint and dignity, Soso Tham shines a light on the corrupt violence of colonialism and the coercive complicity that it engenders when he writes:

> A flatterer adept at placating egos
> Swelling the hide of the sun-eating toad
> And when like a leech she measures each step
> Souls shrivelled by fear stand mutely and watch

Reading Hujon's compelling translation in an era of political turmoil and ecological collapse, Soso Tham takes the form of an Indigenous intellectual and thought leader, calling out for action, resistance, hope and decolonial love:

> Around the world we search for Light
> Yet scorn the light that shines at home

Soso Tham offers us a vision of a more equitable and just world, in which:

> No tax from land flows into his coffers
> For land is common, land bequeathed
> The subjects, you see, are the lords of the land

In Soso Tham's world—a world for which we must all strive—the rights and traditional knowledge of the world's First Peoples are honoured. In the sensibility of our current times, I am reminded of the United Nations Declaration on the Rights of Indigenous Peoples (UNDRIP) when Soso Tham writes of:

> Boundaries defined, rights respected
> Trespass a taboo remaining unbroken

Hujon notes that "Soso Tham came in from the wilderness to carve in words the identity of his people—he made us see, he made us hear, he made us feel and he made us fear". Using her dexterity in both Khasi and English—"Words ripening to a mother tongue"—Hujon's translation lays bare Soso Tham's visualization of the human condition and our extraordinary capacity for hope:

> Man wanders the world to look for a way
> To rebuild restore the Covenant broken
> For light to rise from deep in the dark
> And for an insurgence of song to break out in his heart

While firmly rooted in the ways of his own Khasi community, the transcendent beauty of Soso Tham's writing as transmitted through Janet Hujon's important new translation provides proof of Indigenous resilience and a narrative pathway towards an Indigenous resurgence that is well underway:

> Once again will forests roar
> And stones long still shake to the core
> Days new unknown will surely dawn
> And our homeland ripen as never before

Traditional, ancestral and unceded Musqueam Territory, Vancouver, BC, Canada
March 2018

Khasi hills (2016). Photo by Rpsingh34, CC BY-SA 4.0,
https://commons.wikimedia.org/wiki/File:Khasi_hills.jpg

Acknowledgements

Without Mark Turin this book would still be hovering in the realms of maybe and perhaps. So thank you Mark for your guidance and support which led me to Open Book Publishers where I have received only patience, kindness, and care.

My family in India have been unstinting in their love and belief in me: my uncle Ma Wat, my sister Lily, my aunts Nah Jean, Esther, Margaret and Rose, my cousins, nephews and nieces. I just cannot thank *all* of you enough especially those from whom I sought specific assistance—Alephi, Dee, Elvira, Joan, Linda, Quenda, Raphael, Sandra, Sarah, Sela, Shem and Taflyn. I remember too those who have gone on before. My father who believed in Soso Tham, Meina, my father's siblings, my grandparents, maternal uncles, and great uncles. I still feel the sustaining strength of your love.

I am grateful to Madeline Tham, Kong Alvareen Dkhar and the descendants of U Soso Tham for their faith in me. I hope with all my heart that I have not disappointed you.

I owe a special debt to Bah So Khongsit who shared with me his knowledge of natural history and culture and my respects to Badap Pynnaw and his family, who reminded me that Khasis listen and remember. Kong Maia, thank you to you too for the long-distance help you gave a total stranger.

My school friends: Paromita Lahiri whose soul, deeply marked by her love for the Khasi and Jaiñtia hills, accompanied me on this journey and steadied my nerve. Deepa Majumdar who exhorted me to pursue this dream and Etta Syiem—our long friendship gives added meaning to *ki sngi barim*.

          https://doi.org/10.11647/OBP.0137.15

Here in Cambridge encouragement first came from Gina often fuelled by a glass of wine or two. Colleen, Jane, Gail and Gill—the warmth of your friendship has sustained me throughout encouraging me to keep going. Thank you too for sharing your love of beauty with me and for wanting to know about a green corner in northeast India. Susannah you entered my life at just the right time and showed me the way, and Glenn thank you for being there at the end. Sarah gentle spirit and friend of so many years, you graciously gave to me of your time and skills. And Ruth, to you I offer the birdsong of the Khasi Hills. Ros, Wendy, Habi, Beverly, Linda, Carly, Jenny and Deborah—all of you have carried me along and been happy for me.

Living in Cambridge has brought manifold blessings. The writings of Robert Macfarlane have especially been a source of profound inspiration and encouraged me to walk the old ways again. This city with its interest in other cultures and the vibrant spirit of enquiry has had an undeniable impact on the way I see and write about the world around me. I found myself here.

And finally to my children—Angela and Tom: *nga ieit ia phi*—I love you.

1. Introduction[1]

Then will the rivers of our homeland tear the hills apart[2]

The year is 1935. The event, at least for literature in Khasi, is momentous. A man diminutive in stature but with a voice that cradled the vast soul of his people had decided to do what he knew best. He completed a classic in Khasi literature and the Shillong Printing Works published *The Old Days of the Khasis (Ki Sngi Barim U Hynñiew Trep)*.[3] Soso Tham came in from the wilderness to carve in words the identity of his people—he made us see, he made us hear, he made us feel and he made us fear.

In a land still under British rule this legendary schoolteacher expressed a weary frustration with the English texts he had taught his students year after year. He declared that from now on "he would do it himself". And so he did. An oral culture for whom, in 1841, Thomas Jones of the Welsh Presbyterian Mission had devised a script, now had a scribe whose work expresses a profound love for his homeland and an unwavering pride in the history of his tribe—a history kept alive in rituals and social customs and in fables and legends handed down by generations of storytellers.

Soso Tham refused to believe that a people with no evidence of a written history was without foundation or worth. He set out to compile in verse shared memories of the ancient past—*ki sngi barim*—presenting

---

1   Some of the ideas in the Introduction have appeared in articles I submitted to the *Shillong Times* (Meghalaya) and in a paper entitled 'Surviving Change' which I presented at a conference organised by Lady Keane College, Shillong, in August 2014.

2   Closing line in Soso Tham's Preface to *Ki Sngi Barim U Hynñiew Trep*.

3   Published in Shillong in 1936.

          https://doi.org/10.11647/OBP.0137.01

his people with their own mythology depicting a social and moral universe still relevant to the present day. For him the past is not a dark place but a source of Light, of Enlightenment. It may lie buried but it is not dead, and when discovered will provide the reason for its continued survival. *Ki Sngi Barim U Hynñiew Trep* is the lyrical result of dedicated devotion. It is an account of how Seven Clans—*U Hynñiew Trep*—came down to live on this earth. Tham tells us how

> Groups into a Nation grew
> Words ripening to a mother tongue
> Manifold adherents, one bonding Belief
> Ceremonial dances, offerings of joy, united by a common weave,
> Laws and customs slowly wrought
> Bound this Homeland into one[4]

Not content to be the passive, unquestioning recipient of literary output and thought imposed by a foreign ruling power, Soso Tham decided to write in his native Khasi *and* about his own culture. Although he had embraced Christianity and imbibed Hellenic influences through his reading of English poetry, writing in Khasi expressed his resistance to the dominance of English—for surely, did not the Muse also dwell in his homeland? Creativity, he declared, is not the prerogative of any one culture. With the Himalayan foothills as a backdrop, winding rivers silvering the landscape, and hollows of clear pools and hillside springs, Tham points out that Khasis too have their own Bethel and Mount Parnassus and their own sources of inspiration from which to drink like Panora and Hippocrene in ancient Greece. His dalliance in the literature of distant lands had led him home.

But in throwing off his colonial yoke to mark out an independent path, Tham did so with no trace of chauvinism. His affinity with the Romantics cannot be ignored. While he worked on his articulation of a Khasi vision, Tham remained alive to the gentle unifying truths of human experience and this can be seen in his translations of William Wordsworth's poems into Khasi.

---

4   *Ka Persyntiew* (The Flower Garden), in *Ki Sngi Barim U Hynñiew Trep.*

For reasons of accessibility the nightingale (*The Solitary Reaper*) becomes the local *"kaitor"*,[5] the violet ("Lucy": *She dwelt among the Untrodden Ways*) becomes the *"jami-iang"*,[6] and isn't it just serendipitous that Wordsworth's Cuckoo should so fit Soso Tham's like a glove? This is because her call is heard in the Khasi Hills as it is in the Lake District. So when Tham addresses the bird as "queen of this land of peace" I feel he has not mistranslated the line "Or but a wandering voice?" but has chosen instead to give this spirit of the woods "a local habitation and a name". The Khasification of the cuckoo is complete and a mutual recognition of the need to cherish what we have is established. Perhaps Wordsworth did us a favour, for without his poem Khasis may have never benefited from Tham's translation thus opening our ears and hearts to this denizen haunting our woods.

Poignant sadness in the face of beauty lost or just out of reach, so moving in Keats' *Ode to a Nightingale*, is also felt in *Ki Sngi Barim*: inevitable perhaps in a piece recalling the past amidst a perilous present. Keats is therefore a gentle presence in Tham's work, for listen:

> High on the pine the *Kairiang* sings[7]
> About the old the long lost past,
> Sweetness lies just out of reach
> And such the songs I too will sing[8]
>
> Stars of truth once shone upon
> The darkness of our midnight world
> Oh *Da-ia-mon*, Oh Pen of Gold
> Put down all that there is to know
> Awaken and illuminate
> Before the dying of the light[9]

Furthermore, scenes from a Hellenic past in Keats' *Ode on a Grecian Urn* dovetail neatly with the Khasi homeland where forces of nature each had their own deity. *Ki Sngi Barim* testifies to the ancient Khasi belief

---

5   Himalayan Treepie (*Dendrocitta formosae*), now endangered.

6   Sapphire Berry (*Symplocos Paniculata*).

7   Chestnut-backed Laughing Thrush (*Garrulax nuchalis*) also threatened by habitat loss.

8   *Ka Persyntiew* (The Flower Garden), in *Ki Sngi Barim*.

9   *Ka Pyrthei Mariang* (The Natural World), in *Ki Sngi Barim*.

that the green hills, forests, valleys and tumbling waterfalls are guarded
or haunted by their own patron deities and spirits. Reverence or fear
has traditionally served to protect the natural world. Soso Tham himself
might well have asked:

> What leaf-fringed legend haunts about thy shape
> Of deities of mortals or of both
> In Tempe or the dales of Arcady?...

With their own world of sacred ritual and sacrifice Khasis would also
have understood:

> Who are these coming to the sacrifice?
> To what green altar, O mysterious priest
> Lead'st thou that heifer lowing at the skies
> And all her silken flanks with garlands drest?[10]

Discovering the resonances between the English literary canon and
Khasi poetry has undoubtedly been a source of pleasure because
for me they underline the human stories we all tell. But this was not
necessarily Soso Tham's intention. What he wanted to do was to correct
a gross misconception that still scars and skews the way Khasis look
at themselves *vis-à-vis* western culture. His aim was to rebuild and
restore cultural pride. Recounting the carefully laid down rules of social
conduct, the heated durbars where systems of governance were debated
and established, and the fierce fighting spirit of fabled warriors, Tham
challenges the derogatory labelling of his people as mere "collectors of
heads" or "uncouth jungle dwellers" incapable of sensitive thought and
action.

> Once Great Minds did wrestle with thought
> To strengthen the will, to toughen the nerve
> Once too in parables they spoke they taught
> In public durbar or round the family hearth
> In search of a king, a being in whom
> The hopes of all souls could blossom and fruit

---

10   John Keats, *Ode on a Grecian Urn*, ll:5–7 and ll:31–34.

and

> Boundaries defined, rights respected
> Trespass a taboo remaining unbroken
> Equal all trade, fairness maintained
> Comings and goings in sympathy in step
> Welfare and woe of common concern
> Concord's dominion on the face of the earth[11]

What the poet constantly underlines is that a homeland and a way of life that has survived for centuries cannot be dismissed as insignificant—his ancestors were accurate readers of the writing on the land heeding the lessons and warnings inscribed on "wood and stone".[12] It is this wisdom that accounts for the continued existence of a unique people who, until relatively recently, lived life in tune with their natural surroundings and in sympathy with one another. This is why when Soso Tham renders in words the inspiring beauty of his homeland he does so with profound love and reverence, declaring with absolute conviction:

> Look East, look West, look South, look North
> A land beloved of the gods

With a pride so touching in its childlike certainty he expects no dissent when he asks:

> Will the high Himalaya
> Ever turn away from her
> Pleasure garden, fruit and flower
> Where young braves wander, maidens roam
> Between the Rilang and Kupli[13]
> This is the land they call their home[14]

To fully appreciate why Soso Tham is *the* voice of his people, one needs to know how Khasis respond to the world around them, and we must profoundly reflect upon this if we are to piece together again the

---

11 *Ka Meirilung* (Gentle Motherland), in *Ki Sngi Barim*.
12 *Ki Symboh Ksiar* (Grains of Gold).
13 The names of rivers in the Khasi and Jaiñtia Hills respectively.
14 *Ka Persyntiew* (The Flower Garden), in *Ki Sngi Barim*.

shattered vessel of our cultural confidence. Here I recall what was for me a blinding flash in my understanding of the workings of my mother tongue. Years ago while we were travelling on the London Underground, my cousin made the following observation about an elevator carrying the city's crowds. In Khasi she said: "*Ni, sngap ba ka ud*". This would be the equivalent of saying: "Oh dear! Listen to her moan". Simply because the old grimy elevator had been assigned the status of a human being and specifically that of a woman—"*ka*"—I immediately empathised with "her" suffering. In English the elevator would normally have been referred to as "it", and I am convinced that my imaginative reaction to *it* would have been bland if not altogether non-existent.

On that day I rediscovered the creative roots of my mother tongue. I was reminded that not only do Khasis see living beings, natural forces and inanimate objects as either male or female, but they also endow them with human qualities and feelings. It is this innate poetic tendency that makes the world come *alive* for every Khasi and no one exemplifies this better than Soso Tham. So when he writes about the great storms that batter Sohra, we are left in no doubt that here we are dealing with a living breathing entity, human in essence but with far greater power to awe:

> So the waterfalls threaten and the rivers they growl
> They sink to the plains and they smother the reed
> They banish wild boar who have ruled unopposed
> For that is the way our mighty rains roll
>
> Rivers turn to the left and advance on the right
> They collide with and devour whatever's in sight
> Small islands appear as rice fields are sunk
> The might of the Surma gives the Brahma a fright[15]

Tham's words beat in time to the tempo of the natural world with which he so closely identifies, so that the storm lives through the poet and the poet lives through the storm. The poet *is* the storm. The vivid

---

15   *Ki Kshaid ba Rymphum* (Cascades of Joy), in *Ka Duitara Ksiar*. The Surma is a river in Bangladesh; Brahma is the mighty Brahmaputra (son of Brahma) which flows through Assam.

description provides an insight into what informs the hill person's view of the natural world—this being the ability to respond with both awe and enthusiasm to the might and capriciousness of Nature. For a Khasi to underestimate the significance of perceiving, evaluating and identifying the effects of the natural world on them would be dangerous if not fatal. Yes we can delight in the Khasi flair for story*telling* seen in Tham's descriptions of gentle charm, sweeping majesty and lively engagement, but it is more important to heed the passages inspiring fearful dread. In a land burgeoning with promise and flowing with contentment the sonorous toll of doom is never ever totally muted. Then and even more so now that sense of foreboding cannot be ignored.

In the process of translating I came across the word "*tluh*" which Tham used in connection with his first poetic breakthrough when he was translating the English poem *Drive the Nail Aright Boys* into Khasi. I had to look up the word because it does not form part of my everyday use of Khasi. When I found out that "*tluh*" is "a tree—the fibres of which are used to make ropes, or improvise head-straps, strings"—I felt both enlightened and apprehensive. I felt enlightened because I realised that a whole world of Khasi knowledge and expertise lay in just that one word. But elation was soon replaced by dread.

In his book *Wildwood: A Journey Through Trees* Roger Deakin mourns the fact that "woods have been suppressed by motorways and the modern world, and have come to look like the subconscious of the landscape [...] The enemies of woods", he says, "are always the enemies of culture and humanity"[16]... and this is what made me apprehensive. Had I not come across the word "*tluh*", I would never have discovered the world to which it refers. How much more do I not know? How much more have we lost? I therefore marvel not only at our poet's appropriate choice of image but I also value the lesson he points us towards.

Today the Khasi and Jaiñtia Hills form part of Meghalaya, a state in North-East India which came into being following local demand for the recognition of a strongly felt tribal identity. But it is clearly evident that long before this overt political step was taken Soso Tham had

---

16 Roger Deakin, *Wildwood: A Journey Through Trees* (London: Penguin, 2008), Introduction, p. xii.

already addressed the question of identity, carrying with it that sense of rootlessness deeply embedded in the Khasi psyche, a raw wound sensitive to the reminder that "the Other" whom we have encountered in our recorded history has invariably been certain of his or her historical beginnings. This, I feel, accounts for the leitmotif of sadness running through Khasi literary and musical compositions, and the numerous nuanced terms for sadness and regret. Tham speaks for so many when he asks:

> Tell me children of the breaking dawn
> Mother-kite, mother-crow,
> You who circle round the world
> Where the soil from which we sprang?
> For if I could, like you I'd drift
> Down the ends of twelve-year roads![17]

Ki Sngi Barim is both a love letter to his homeland and a troubled and troubling exploration of what makes and sustains that fragile sense of self. He sees the battle for identity being waged on two fronts—against the enemy without and the enemy within. A reading of the work reveals in no uncertain terms that Tham fears the enemy within more than he does the foe without. Tragically this is still the case today. Mineral-rich Meghalaya with its dense forest cover is now a treasure trove being exploited by the rapacious few using tribal "rights" over the land as justification for their actions:

> Man's greed is now a gluttonous sow
> (A pouch engorged about to rip)[18]

Ki Sngi Barim is trenchant social critique told through a trajectory of spiritual questing. Through the converging prisms of Khasi myth and religion, Tham tells the universal story of temptation and man's fall from grace. But despite the poet's despair hope is never totally lost, for the narrative journeys towards the possibility of rejuvenation as we see in the final section *Ka Aïom Ksiar* (Season of Gold):

---

17   *Ka Meirilung* (Gentle Motherland), in *Ki Sngi Barim*.
18   *U Lyoh* (The Cloud), in *Ki Sngi Barim*.

> The Peacock will dance when the Sun returns[19]
> And she will bathe in the Rupatylli[20]
> O Rivers Rilang, Umiam and Kupli[21]
> Sweet songs in you will move inspire
> Land of Nine Roads, pathways of promise[22]
> Where the Mole will strum, the Owl will dance[23]

Spellbound by the beauty of his homeland, the poet steadfastly holds on to his belief that the land that he fiercely cherishes and that inspires his art will once again be a spring of renewal and creativity. Whatever else this translation may achieve, my hope is that the powerful life of an old tradition will reawaken so that when we read we will *hear*:

> The crash of rivers, the thunder of waterfalls
> In the Khasi minstrel's reed-piped-ears
> Where tumult is hushed and silence then ripples
> To the furthest brink of infinite time[24]

Perhaps the human voice will once again reassert its power to empower and change:

> Then once again will forests roar
> And stones long still shake to the core[25]

---

19 A Khasi tale explaining the eyes on the tail of the Peacock who once upon a time lived in the sky with his wife the Sun. But one day as he looked down on the earth below he saw a golden-haired maiden with whom he instantly fell in love. He flew down only to discover that he had been captivated by a field of golden mustard. The foolish peacock was left heartbroken and realised he was doomed to live on earth forever. From that time onwards each morning he danced at sunrise to greet his wife whose tears would fall on his outspread tail and became those eyes on the tail of the Peacock.

20 The Surma now in Bangladesh. Here it is compared to a necklace of solid silver.

21 Rivers in the Khasi and Jaiñtia Hills.

22 The Khasi word "*lad*" means both path or road as well as opportunity, so to translate the phrase "*Khyndai lad*" solely into Nine Roads would not necessarily imply opportunity. Hence my addition of "pathways of promise" in order to convey the local extended meaning of the word.

23 Both the Mole and the Owl participate in a dance described in the legend about the Sacred Cave where the Sun hid her light to punish living creatures for casting doubt on her relationship with her brother the Moon. See Chapter 3, pp. 21–22.

24 *U Lum Shillong* (Shillong Peak), in *Ka Duitara Ksiar*.

25 From *Ka Persyntiew* (The Flower Garden), in *Ki Sngi Barim*.

Elephant falls, Shillong (2010). Photo by Joshua Singh, CC BY 2.0,
https://www.flickr.com/photos/joshuasingh/4660903646

2. A Short Biographical Note

Soso Tham, 1873–1940

In 1841 a Welshman named Thomas Jones arrived in the Khasi Hills of North East India, bringing with him the message of the Christian gospel. It was to better serve the aims of his mission that Jones decided to use the Roman script in order to set down the Khasi language in writing. But Jones was also "adamant about the need to teach the Khasis to read and write their own language first before attempting to learn English".[1] So began a re-drawing of the cultural map of these hills and several decades later, Soso Tham, as ardent student and inspiring teacher, deepened the lines on that map. In one of his letters to his son working in the British Army Office (Mesopotamia) during the First World War the poet writes in English: "In one way it is only what we write that matters in life. So the more you express yourself in letters the better."[2]

Ki Sngi Barim U Hynñiew Trep[3] still stands as the final flowering of Soso Tham's literary genius, but his facility in the use of English and his intense pride in the wealth of his mother tongue resulted in his other works in Khasi, as well as translations from English to Khasi. These include *Ki Phawer u Aesop* (*Aesop's Fables*) first published in 1920, *Ka Duitara Ksiar ne ki Poetry Khasi* (*The Golden Duitara, or Khasi Poems*) in

---

1   Andrew J. May, *Welsh Missionaries and British Imperialism: The Empire of Clouds in Northeast India* (Manchester and New York: Manchester University Press, 2012), p. 139.

2   A. A. Dkhar, *Na U Kpa Sha U Khun* ([Letters] from a Father to his Son) (Shillong, Shandora Press, 2013), p. 12.

3   Soso Tham, *Ki Sngi Barim U Hynñiew Trep* (Shillong: Shillong Printing Works, 1936). A more recent edition was published in Shillong by Primrose Gatphoh in 1976.

     https://doi.org/10.11647/OBP.0137.02

1931[4] and *Ka Jingim U Trai Jong Ngi* (a translation of Charles Dickens's *The Life of our Lord*),[5] which appeared in 1936 after *Ki Sngi Barim*. He successfully bridged the gap between the old and the new.

Tham died in 1940, leaving behind a body of work that speaks volumes about a man who, against all odds, could draw blood from the proverbial stone. The death of his beloved wife meant he was left alone to care for his five young children. As if this tragedy was not enough he then had to bear the loss of his only daughter, an experience he likened to being "whipped by the tempest". His letters to his son contain frequent references to his continuing struggle to make ends meet. But despite all the hardship Tham's tenacity of spirit and sense of purpose never wavered. He never lost the will to find the words to convey his fierce pride in the homeland that made bright his vision and nurtured his spirit.

---

4   Soso Tham, *Ka Duitara Ksiar ne ki Poetry Khasi*, 8th ed., rev. and enl. (*The Golden Duitara*) (Shillong: Primrose Gatphoh, 1972).

5   Soso Tham, *Ka Jingim U Trai Jong Ngi*, 2nd ed. ([n.p.], 1936), available at https://archive.org/details/in.ernet.dli.2015.464546

3. Khasi Folktales About Darkness and Light

Long, long ago before anyone can remember, there was a Time we now call the Ancient Past. She holds and protects all the days that once were young but have now grown old, that once were new, but now have aged. No one has ever seen her, but we all know her. Khasis call her *Myndai* or *Ki Sngi Barim*—the days that make up Time long gone.

In that Time lived peace and harmony guarded by the Seven Families, who, in answer to the prayers of the Great Spirit of Earth, *Ka Ramew*, were sent down by God to care for all living creatures and forces—rivers, trees, animals, flowers, fruit. From their grass-thatched homes (*Ki Trep*) the Seven (*Hynñiew*) went forth, increased and multiplied. These Seven Families are the first clans, the mothers and fathers of all Khasis today. *They* are the *Hynñiew Trep*.

Although they lived on earth, the *Hynñiew Trep* were able to visit the other Nine Clans who still lived in Heaven. They could do this because there was a Golden Ladder bridging the space between heaven and earth. This ladder was on the sacred mountain—*U Lum Sohpet Bneng*—a mountain that stood at the centre of the world and was therefore known as the navel of heaven—*u sohpet*. The Golden Ladder was the umbilical cord linking terrestrial beings to their celestial beginnings.

So for a time all on earth was as God had ordained until the Seven Clans forgot their duty to their Creator and to one another—to *Tip Blei, Tip Briew*—to know and honour God and each other. Swallowed by Greed they were reborn as creatures who no longer saw with the eyes of contentment. They no longer revered the might of the great mountains

 https://doi.org/10.11647/OBP.0137.03

and waterways that protected and fed the green world they lived in. They feverishly took from the earth, refusing to listen to her cries of protest. Finally, exhausted, the earth fell silent.

God looked down in despair at his chosen people. Custodians appointed to care for creation had broken their word. Anger grew in his heart. He turned his face away and destroyed the Golden Ladder. From that day onwards the *Hynñiew Trep* never again knew the freedom of being allowed to walk in heaven.

Their misfortune increased when a monstrous tree—the *Diengïei*—began to push its way through the soil. The tree grew and grew until its branches covered the face of the earth: a canopy so dense that not even the strength of the sun's rays could push through. The land lay dying yet the *Diengïei* kept growing. Stricken with terror the people seized their blades and axes and began to hack at the solid trunk. They knew that without light they too would die. Every evening they returned to their homes having left a gaping wound in the trunk and always determined to return the next day to finish their task. But each morning they returned to find the wound had healed. The trunk looked as good as new. What was going on?

Worn out and weary in spirit the people looked at each other in despair. Then suddenly in the silence they heard the voice of the *Phreit*, a tiny wren-like creature—"If you promise to spare me some grain after every harvest, I will tell you why all your efforts are in vain." At first the people refused to believe her, but seeing no other explanation for this mystery, they agreed to grant the little bird's request. "From this day onwards" they said, "You and all your descendants will always have a share of our harvest."

And this is what the *Phreit* told them: "Every night after you return to your homes, the Tiger arrives and licks the cut clean. By morning the tree is renewed and the gash is sealed. So no matter how hard you hack you will not be able to fell the *Diengïei*." The words of the little bird plunged the people into an even deeper darkness. Then she spoke again: "But I know a way out of this." Immediately they looked up. "Tell us," they implored, "Tell us little bird!" "This is what you must do. This evening, before you go home, leave an axe in the wound of the tree. Make sure the blade is facing outwards". The people did as they were told. In the morning they returned to find a blood-stained blade and the tree unhealed. It was not long before the mighty *Diengïei* came crashing down. Light and life returned to earth and the people remembered to keep their promise to the *Phreit*.

But one day darkness once again returned to the earth and this is how it happened:

For a while the people remembered their suffering. They kept the laws and looked out for each other. With the return of peace and harmony they decided to celebrate life in a dance to which the Sun, her brother the Moon, and all living creatures on earth were invited. Arriving late after her day's work, the Sun abandoned herself to the happiness of the moment as she danced with her brother in an arena by now emptied of all other dancers.

Suddenly a hum like the moaning of bees and wasps rose into the air: murmurs of disapproval from the crowd that watched the siblings move in absolute surrender to the joyous freedom of the dance. Doubts darkened the onlookers' minds—should a brother and sister move together in such blatant unison? Had they broken the most sacred of all taboos? The clamour grew louder and finally became so unbearable that the Sun decided to leave, but not before she had vented her rage on the crowd for their harsh and hurtful words. "Never again", she said, "will I bring you my blessings of warmth and light." With those ominous words hanging in the air she left and plunged into a deep dark cave—*Ka Krem Lamet Ka Krem Latang*. Because the people saw evil where there was only joy and shame where it did not exist, they were punished. And once again human beings had to look for a way out of Darkness and into Light.

Time became an unending stretch of all-enveloping night in which the people were lost. Filled with remorse they pleaded with the Sun but she refused to emerge. Who could they find to placate the enraged Sun? Then Hope came in the form of the lowly Rooster—an unadorned creature who hid in shame from other living beings. If the people draped him in beautiful silks, he said, he would feel confident enough to stand before the nurturer of life and bow before her flaming throne to plead their cause. The people agreed. He was garbed in the finest and richest of silks—the fabric reserved for the rich and for royalty. When they had finished he had been transformed. Turquoise melted into the dark blue of night. Carmine, terracotta and gold fired the gloss of darkness while grey and white flowed in gentle stripes. And as the ultimate mark of distinction a red crest was placed on his head. Before them stood a prince!

He set off on his long journey. Often he took shelter and rested in the branches of the rubber tree and the venerable oak. Finally he arrived at the entrance of the *Krem Lamet* and in his many-splendoured robes he faced the Sun. With a voice clear and true he said: "I stand here before you O Great Being to seek your forgiveness for a people who now know they acted in ignorance and have repented. I have come here to offer my life in exchange for their freedom from this punishment. Return to their midst, Great One, restore light to their lives." Moved by his simple request and selflessness, the Sun not only relented but also spared the Rooster's life.

The Rooster bowed in humble thanksgiving and said: "From now on, O Great Being, I will remind myself and the world of the mercy you have shown us. At the beginning of each day I will announce your coming with a bugle of three calls so that all living creatures will know you have returned in order that the earth might live."

As a token of remembrance for the kindness shown to the Rooster by the rubber tree, the oak, and the leaf (*Lamet*), these three are always included in Khasi rituals, commemorating forever the significance of Gratitude and Memory in the lives of the Khasis.

4. *Ki Symboh Ksiar*–Grains of Gold

The opening lines of *Ki Sngi Barim U Hynñiew Trep* explain why Soso Tham decided to compose his *magnum opus*. Saddened by the fact that his people continued to look elsewhere for inspiration while failing to appreciate the cultural wealth into which they are born, he set out to reclaim and record the past—*ki sngi barim*—that survives in myth. He tells of a time now lost to us when the Khasi and *Pnar* people, who call themselves *U Hynñiew Trep,* came to be here on earth. This is the "Once upon a time" section of that story referring to legends and tales told and shared, of a common heritage of the imagination that has held a people together.

Grains of Gold

> We scour the world in search of light
> Know not the light within our land
> How long ago far back in time
> Our ancients did new worlds create
> For then the *Seven* lived apart[1]
> Impenetrable heavy was the dark

---

1   "The Seven Original Ancestors". See Chapter 3, pp. 19–20.

https://doi.org/10.11647/OBP.0137.04

Among the Stars the Sun and Moon
On hills and forests, spirits roamed,
Man and Beast, the Tiger, *Thlen*[2]
United by a common tongue
Before the grim macabre took hold
They worshipped then the One True God

The Spoken Word was then revered
The humble *Phreit* was honoured, fed,[3]
Hard they toiled from dawn to dusk
Knowledge cached within the womb[4]
From where our legends sprang to life
And wingéd sprites sung into being

Of signs and symbols some did speak,
"From here," some said, "Came forth the *Thlen*;"
"Sin and Taboo? Whence that flood?"
"From here", they cried, "From *Lum Diengïei*:"[5]
But of the One, no one had doubts
Why He was called "*U Sohpet Bneng*"[6]

Of God and Sin, so too of Truth
In parables as one they spoke
Old voices tell of visions draped
By *Ka Rngai* for all mankind[7]
Some stars live on in scattered gardens
The rest have drowned in forests deep

---

2   The Giant Snake which promised wealth to his worshippers, and had to be kept happy by human sacrifices.

3   Munia, Spotted Munia, Red Munia etc. A little wren-like bird, which helped mankind. See Chapter 3, pp. 20–21.

4   Khasis believe they lost their script in a great flood. The Khasi thought his precious script would be safe in his mouth but he swallowed it as he battled the raging waters.

5   The hill on which stood the monstrous tree (*Ka Diengïei*) that covered the earth—a sign of God's displeasure (See Chapter 3, pp. 20–21).

6   "The Navel of Heaven" (See Chapter 3, pp. 19–20).

7   "*Ka*" denotes the feminine (as "*U*" denotes the masculine). "*Rngai*" is a word with shadowy connotations pointing to spectres, phantoms, the unreal yet powerfully real in the potency of its effect. So here "*Ka Rngai*" is a powerful female force.

To banish Sin, to bear the yoke
In the *Sacred Cave* far back in time[8]
The fearless Cockerel rose upright
"I wait the word from God above."
A Creed was born—its rites revered
By children of the *Hynñiew Trep*

Tears from a mother's pain-wracked heart
Shadow the bier which bears her son,
Fingers strum, recall the tale
The legend of the noble Stag
The rusted Arrow piercing deep
The rushing flood of bitter tears[9]

Signs once clear on boulder rock
Remain unread, obscured, weed-choked,
Where Orators Thinkers once declaimed
Spoke in tongue unknown to us,
Yet hilltop stark and sheltered shade
Wood and Stone still speak to man

Ancient race—*Khasi* and *Pnar*
Ranged across the earth's arm span
Hidden light waits to be found
In modest thatch and humble roost
To help us peel, push back the dark
Restore the light from days of old

---

8 The sacred cave into which the sun retreated, angered by the aspersions cast on her by those who attended the Dance of Thanksgiving (See Chapter 3, pp. 21–22).

9 This is a reference to what is known as "The Khasi Lament"—a song of grief pouring out from a mother's heart when she discovers the body of her wayward son who, against her wishes, had strayed too far from home. He dies from the wound inflicted by an arrow. Archery is still a common pastime in the Khasi and Jaiñtia Hills where the Khasi and *Pnar* (Jaiñtia) people live.

Around the world we search for Light
Yet scorn the light that shines at home
The glorious past will dawn again
When seams of lustre-lost we mine
The seed of light his vibrant root
Into the Past he pierces deep

Gleam of sky on rock we'll see
When sun-showers stop and fade away
Dark dense clouds retreat in fear
As the rainbow rises in the sky;
Libations pour, O Golden Pen
Emblazon with colour the blinding dark!

 Listen to an audio recording of the poem at
https://doi.org/10.11647/OBP.0137.16

5. *Ka Persyntiew*– The Flower Garden

Evocative of Eden, this section describes the haunting beauty of Tham's homeland. Although the Khasi and Jaiñtia Hills have been plundered for their forest and mineral wealth there still remain large tracts that are heartbreakingly beautiful, able to stir wonder today as they did in the distant past. That poignant longing for what once was is as acute now as it was when Soso Tham composed his masterpiece.

The Flower Garden

On bracing hillcrests, shielded lee
Refreshed I walk, alone reflect
Upon my homeland's darkened heart,
Then under every thatch I find
Scattered grains of thought profound
Alive in pools of haunting tears

Golden grains forgotten old
Abandoned random still remain
As when in fresh fields left behind
Rice potato millet yam
Each with a bygone tale to tell
Of what was sown, of what has been

Translation and Notes © Janet Hujon, CC BY 4.0   https://doi.org/10.11647/OBP.0137.05

The bird still calls within the wood
The kite she casts her eye afar
Melodies I weave to make a song.
Swift I turn in an eye's quick blink
To shake awake from biers extinct
The Ancient Past of the *Hynñiew Trep*

Once this land was still untouched
Unpeopled empty pristine void
Then the *Seven* first came down
To loosen the soil, to plough the land,
Filling gardens with flowers, orchards with fruit
A land where the human race could thrive

To far-flung corners soon they spread
Their yield increased their harvests rich
Fruit plantations, betel groves[1]
Grains of gold strung to adorn.
The wilderness rumbled, boulders crashed
Tumult echoed, shook the land

Groups into a Nation grew
Words ripening to a mother tongue
Manifold adherents, one bonding Belief
Ceremonial dances, offerings of joy, united by a
    common weave,
Laws and customs slowly wrought
Bound this Homeland into one

The world was then a different place
Birds soared freely, beasts at peace
Out in the open or concealed from sight
Flowers with ease communed with man,

---

1   The betel nut is central to Khasi social and religious culture. The serving and
     chewing of betel/areca nuts (*kwai*) along with a betel leaf of the Piperaceae family
     (*tympew*) and a dab of slaked lime (*shun*) is never absent from a Khasi home, so
     much so that a folk tale grew around a tragic friendship involving the three. See
     Bijoya Sawian, 'How Paan Came Into Existence', in her *Khasi Myths, Legends and
     Folk Tales* (Shillong: Ri Khasi Press, 2006), pp. 12–14.

Submerged beneath the tangle-weed
Thirty-thoughts-have-sprung-from-two... where quiet
  blooms *U Tiew Dohmaw*[2]

Peacocks danced with wild abandon
Wild boar rolled in cooling mud
In deep dark pools *Sher* supple dart[3]
Under sheltering fern the doe lies quiet
The courting call of *U Rynniaw*[4]
Lulled nodding monkey, capped langur

Grazing stags on tender green
Sleeping tigers in the gloom
Cooling hills warm days just right
While wild nymphs splash in waterfalls.
Look East, look West, look South, look North
A land beloved of the gods

High on the pine the *Kairiang* sings[5]
About the old the long lost past,
Sweetness lies just out of reach
And such the songs I too will sing.
Then once again will forests roar
And stones long still shake to the core

---

2   *Anoectochilus brevilabris* belongs to the group of Jewel Orchids. *Tiew Dohmaw* literally means the flower which kisses the stone. This tiny flower, with its velvety leaves, blooms against boulders and rocks in the Khasi Hills, usually halfway up a gorge—hence it is not often easily visible. The sight of such vulnerable beauty, of fragile softness against enduring hardness, inspires the poet to contemplate this natural phenomenon. Hence "Thirty-thoughts-have-sprung-from-two". Man and plant commune in silence.

3   *Lepidocephalichthys guntea*. A small fish found in streams and in paddy fields. The full name in Khasi is "*shersyngkai*"—I have used the shortened version. *Syngkai* means waist, so the name evokes the supple twisting movements made by these fish as they twist and dart in the water.

4   Greater Racket-Tailed Drongo. In a folktale he is cast as King of the Kingdom of Shade and falls in love with *Ka Sohlygngem* (Ashy Wood Pigeon) whose parents warn her against marrying a rich man. Unwilling to cause her parents any more grief, the selfless *Rynniaw* leaves and flies away. Even today the cries of the *Sohlyngngem* haunt the forest shade as she searches for her lost love.

5   Chestnut-backed laughing thrush (*Garrulax nuchalis*) now endangered, but once common in Sohra, where Soso Tham was born.

Will the high Himalaya
Ever turn away from her
Pleasure garden, fruit and flower
Where young braves wander, maidens roam
Between the Rilang and Kupli[6]
This is the land they call their home.

 Listen to an audio recording of the poem at
https://doi.org/10.11647/OBP.0137.17

---

6   The names of rivers in the Khasi and Jaiñtia Hills respectively.

6. *Pyrthei Mariang–*
The Natural World

The natural descriptions here are just as beautiful as in the preceding section but the poignancy is sharpened because they are set down in a mood of sad recollection. This is why the poet begins this section with a plea for inspiration as he seeks to fulfill his task of restoring the wonder and virtues of the past. This long look into the past from a present that is found to be wanting, creates a seam of tender pain which runs right though the composition springing from the tension that exists between what was, what is and what still might be. This in fact is a feature of a composition illustrating how the past, the present and the future coexist in a relationship of troubling unease. The poet goes in search of *U Sohpet Beneng* who represents the now severed umbilical cord that once linked Heaven and Earth and is "the He whom I love" now lost to humankind. *U Sohpet Beneng* is thus shown to be the mediator between God and Man.

The Natural World

Stars of truth once shone upon
The darkness of our midnight world
Oh <u>Da</u>-*ia-mon*, Oh Pen of Gold[1]
Put down all that there is to know
Awaken and illuminate
Before the dying of the light

---

1   Khasi pronunciation of the word "diamond" which I have retained to sustain the rhythm.

    https://doi.org/10.11647/OBP.0137.06

O lift the gloom and lead me on
Away from shadows cast by trees,
Along the paths of silver streams
Draughts of wind-fresh I will drink
On cascade summit, abyss verge,
Oh where is He, He whom I love![2]

Gradual was the dawn of light
In that age of innocence
Truth seeped slowly through our ears
Those echo-chambers built of stone
Scenic splendour in the sky
We took our time to see the sun

Roused by gentle springtime winds
The sun begins her journey down
Footprints green she leaves behind
In open fields and hidden shade
Life was pure, we were held safe
As children in our parents' laps

Just before the Autumn calls
Insects, birds break into song
Steeped in joy the land, the living
And tranquil rests the mind of man
Then surged that flow of gold-glint tears
Its headspring though... he could not find

Perhaps the Spirit Queen of Earth
Sees with vision bright and true
How stars from teardrops congregate
In waters of an endless ocean.
Into the Garden, God steps down
Beguiling time away with man[3]

---

2   From the point of view of those who retain the indigenous faith, this is a reference
      to a Saviour who will restore the Golden Ladder between Heaven and Earth. From
      the point of the Christian Khasi this is a reference to Christ. Soso Tham was a
      devout Christian.

3   An approximate translation of the Khasi expression *"iaid kai"*. The adverb *"kai"*
      suggests a mood that has no single English word as an equivalent and yet is very

On distant peaks they linger
Those children of the gods
Their eyes rest soft on earth's great rivers
As they listen to the *Riyar*'s song[4]
Peace contentment reigned supreme
Before the Heavenly Cord was cleaved[5]

Our streams and rivers flowed along
Well-traced paths on boulder rock
So too the Golden Ladder scaled
Movement safe from dawn to dusk
Night a time of sound repose
Day was mother to a virtuous race

Under a roof soot-sodden thick
Night plucks the strings—*kynting-ting-ting*
A blush burns deep on a girlish cheek
Intense the gaze of the perfect moon[6]
Dried fish and rice my mother served
What joy replete in humble fare

---

much a part of Khasi identity, and it concerns me that in a world fixated on status and material success, we might be losing this trait. We have banished ourselves from Eden to enter the rat race whatever the cost. *"Kai"* possesses a sense of pleasurable purposelessness. *"Ïaid kai"* (rambling, strolling in the manner of a flaneur); *"shongkai"* (sit around), *"peitkai"* (just looking), *"leitkai"* (a leisurely outing) and so on. Perhaps "hanging out" or "chill" best approaches the feeling contained in the word although both these words indicate an attitude that involves premeditation or conscious choice and therefore do not possess the relaxed spontaneity of the easy going *"kai"* which has a connotation of freedom to roam, to look, to relax—"for free"—in a world that is not bound by the demands of time. Even the act of voicing the gliding diphthong *"ai"* is a long drawn out process expanding time and gently seductive. So the fact that God came down to *"ïaid kai"* in this plausible Eden in the Khasi hills underlines a sympathy for natural harmony that permeates our being and I hope will not be totally erased from our troubled state gripped by the tightening coils of corruption vividly described in *Ki Sngi Barim* for yes, as in the Biblical Eden, Tham's *Ka Persyntiew* (The Flower Garden) also shelters a dangerous embodiment of evil—the serpent.

4   A songbird in the Sohra region.
5   See Chapter 3, pp. 19–20, when the Golden Ladder between heaven and earth was cut.
6   No matter that the Moon is male in Khasi, the beauty of this heavenly body is celebrated as in other cultures. A handsome young man is compared to a perfect moon who has bloomed for fourteen midnights.

Slander shunned, deceit abhorred
Truth in its prime stood resolute
The skies a clear cerulean blue,
Gently passed that time of gold
When those who trod the skin of earth
Were all held fast in God's embrace

Then the land was free of taint
In sun-brief moments ripening swift,
And there amidst the blossom, fruit
The faces of young maidens, men;
If there be other wondrous lands
To them O then do let me fly!

 Listen to an audio recording of the poem at
https://doi.org/10.11647/OBP.0137.18

7. U Lyoh–The Cloud

This is the point to which the preceding sections have been journeying. Here we come upon an utterly bleak apocalyptic scene which Soso Tham fears will replace the green fecundity and harmony of his homeland if Khasis betray the Laws and Truths with which they came into this world. Soso Tham's dramatic description of opportunist worshippers of Mammon is as accurate today as it was then. Imagery from the natural world and Khasi myth powerfully portray the dysfunctional hell to which we are going to descend as a people who are powerless to resist the temptation of worldly wealth. The poet had good reason to be fearful. Evident today are plundered forests, rivers poisoned by the unscientific extraction of coal, exhaustive sand and limestone mining, and hills bulldozed out of shape to create highways to "development" and wealth for a few—the list continues to grow.

The Cloud

Free of want once lived our children
Before the ox betrayed his Maker[1]

---

1   A reference to the folktale where the ox lost his upper teeth for not carrying out God's explicit instructions warning human beings not to be wasteful with their natural resources, more specifically asking them to cook only the required amount of rice so there is nothing left to throw out. On his way to deliver his message to mankind, the ox was plagued by insect bites, an agony finally relieved by a crow alighting on his back to peck and devour the irritants. But hearing about the message the ox had to deliver, the crow was alarmed for she feared her tribe would lose a source of food in the form of rice offerings left at cremation grounds for departed souls (See Chapter 9, verse 7). So she persuaded the ox not to carry out God's bidding. Grateful to the crow the ox agreed. But God was enraged when he found out that the ox had disobeyed, and struck the ox a huge blow knocking out all his upper teeth.

   https://doi.org/10.11647/OBP.0137.07

Fruit ripened red, stalks fleshed with grain,
Each day brim-filled, each palm grain-full
Daylight hours of peaceful toil
Before the virtuous took flight

Courteous speech well-learnt, well-honed
Advice on restless sleep unknown
Laughter rippled, gentle ease
Beneath the solace-shade of trees,
But far away the Eagle King
Saw signs of disquiet, portents of unease

Before the *Diengïei's*[2] cover spread
Moves with stealth the reprobate
Slowly climbs the threatening cloud
Thickening smoke from pyres untended
Obscured the sun from mountain peaks
A tribe abandoned by their God

A swarm of bees without a queen
Wandering, lost, directionless
Criss-crossing blind through open skies,
    stumbling into thickets deep
Nine remain in the House of God
Dispersed on earth were the *Hynñiew Trep*[3]
From heaven estranged — *U Sohpet Bneng*[4] slashed

As he swims through earth's dark waters
Man sinks down to unplumbed depths
To black-hole dread in no-end caves
To deserts parched and wetlands rich
As far as Nine Infernal Tiers
Where all alone he seeks to feel... the spasms of a
    wished-for birth[5]

---

2   See Chapter 3, pp. 20–21.
3   See Chapter 3, pp. 19–20.
4   See *ibid.*
5   To give birth to and thus jettison the evil he carries within himself and thus be
     born anew. Or, to give birth to the Knowledge symbolised by the script he had
     swallowed and lost in the Great Flood.

The serpent's lair within a cave
Its blackness heavy with his stench,
Below—the coils of languorous power
Above stands She!—The Mother of the *Thlen*.[6]
Just such a nest is the human heart
A place where Evil lays her eggs

God looks down and shakes his head
Sees toads and frogs eat Suns and Moons[7]
Humped dwarves, Scorpions, Snakes
Infinite hordes defying count
The Age of Purity has lost her throne
Triumphant the Pasha of the Enslaved

His eyes shut-blind seamed tight with pus,
    his ears no longer can they hear
His children dulled by blunted thought
For Darkness is Queen, and Ignorance rules
Fear and Unease their subjects now,
So wonder not if we should find
Devils mingling with mankind

All that remains is barren rock, fertility long since
    washed away
Settlers, settlements ruined destroyed
The pleasure garden once so loved
Forsaken now, she's left bereft,
Days of peace must surely end
When the dark cloud drops and shrouds the light

Slow inch by inch the toad consumes
The sun gripped tight in her clamping jaws
While poverty, hunger, suffering, woe
Hereditary taint suck clean away... the marrow
    from the land.

---

6   See p. 24, n. 2.
7   This is a reference to the old Khasi explanation for an eclipse. Khasis believed the
     phenomenon was caused by a giant toad or frog in the sky swallowing the sun and
     moon.

In under-floor gloom a seed once thrived
Why now is it pale yellow in the dark?

Infernal beings deprived of sight
Collide and stumble, trample all
The race, the clan begins to shrink
The face made foul by ugliness
With honour dying in the heart
The face has lost its source of light

And will so appear forever more
For the indwelling Soul has taken flight.[8]
The blacksmith's wares in full display
But was hammer-strike on anvil heard?
In murky gloom among the rafters, the intruder waits
    for night to fall
Is there a being more sinister than he hell-bent on
    chicanery?

Broodings foul of ill intent
Increase in strength, convene within
For verily now they are "the gods",
Where hides the Queen[9] of the floundering bee
As sightless now he gropes his way
In a frenzied search for the Goddess Wealth

---

8   "indwelling soul" is my equivalent of the phrase "*ka Rngiew*", different from U
     Rngiew, the embodiment of evil in Chapter 8. The word/concept is difficult to
     translate. It is sometimes likened to an aura or compared to the Greek psyche
     meaning "soul" or "spirit". Khasis believe that every person is endowed with a
     vital life force that waxes and wanes in strength. It is this invisible essence which
     the onlooker senses, and then accordingly tenders respect or heaps derision.

9   Soso Tham uses the word *Kyiaw* (Mother-in-law) but I have used Queen as that
     more accurately aligns with an English sense of what the poet is trying to convey.
     To a Khasi *kyiaw* would make sense from the point of view of the social custom
     where once married the man leaves his maternal home and becomes part of his
     kyiaw's home, where she is traditionally revered as the caring queen of the family.

She who flies through cave and crevice
Rustling through unsightly weeds.
To cities, plains and borderlands[10]
Where man has journeyed to earn a living
Seeking out sustaining grain
Rice the lure, the face assumed by the Goddess Wealth[11]

No longer then can we discern
Waving palms above *Mawïew* gorge[12]
The rising fog has brought its blight
Withering our sense of shame, of right,
Are there voids of darker menace
Than those we call the human heart?

White ants that fly through air and light
Did once emerge from the termite's hole
Like fiendish scourge of hornet, wasp
Who from dark places emigrate,
But Integrity and Honour shun the confines
Of Pandemonium's night[13]

For a fistful of silver men sink their teeth
Tight the clench, unrelenting the grip
Like Mighty Mammon defeated bowed
All are seduced by the Goddess Fair
From heavenly highways lined with gold
To buried seams in Hell's Nine Tiers

---

10   This is the area known as *Lyngngam* in the South West Khasi hills where the people, also known as the *Lyngngam*, are of mixed Khasi and Garo ancestry. Garo is a language of Tibeto-Burman origin while Khasi belongs to the Mon-Khmer family of languages. Soso Tham does use the word *Lyngngam*, but to maintain the rhythmic pace of the line and to convey the connotation of the word *Lyngngam*, I have used "borderlands".

11   To the Khasi there cannot be any substitute for rice as a food staple. A person who goes out to earn their living to feed the family is one who goes in search of rice—the only grain that can provide sustenance and satisfaction!

12   A ravine near Sohra so deep that filling it with soil would be a nigh impossible feat. See also the penultimate stanza in this section where man's greed is compared to "a *Mawïew* gorge" that cannot be filled.

13   Milton's *Paradise Lost* made a deep impression on Soso Tham.

Silver cowries Her brilliant lenses[14]
She blinds the tempted with her dazzling vision
Tapestry threads of tortured logic
Which the gold? Which twist the maggot?
For Falsehood's stature to command respect
She rips the mote from the eye of Truth

"Timidity hobbles adventure", so we are told
Yet renegades run riot respecting no bounds
Hills avalanche, waterholes seethe
"Heat scorches advance, cold freezes retreat"
Rulings judgements exchanges intense
All blinded by the silver slime

The scion dines with rival groups
Purse strings hang lax, no taboo restrains
Where dissension prevails and discord persists
It is there that he seeks to add weight to his gold
While Truth has her abode in the City of God
On the skin of the earth untouched by shame, blatantly
    bulges the purse of man[15]

Man's greed is now a gluttonous sow
(A pouch engorged about to rip)
A flatterer adept at placating egos
Swelling the hide of the sun-eating toad[16]
And when like a leech she measures each step
Souls shrivelled by fear stand mutely and watch

---

14   The Khasis once used cowrie shells as currency in trading activities.

15   Through sheer chance I discovered that the Khasi word *pdok* has two meanings—
     the gall bladder and a purse. Maybe it has more? So another possible translation
     of this line could well be: "Man's gall exposed on the skin of the earth". I feel both
     meanings of the word "gall" feed into Soso Tham's use of the word as conveying
     a totality of experience which accounts for the darkness enveloping the poet's soul
     and contributing to his sense of foreboding.

16   See p. 37, n. 7. This line vividly conveys the image of uncontrollable greed,
     especially if one compares the size of the toad to that of the sun.

The Silver Cowrie is armed with teeth
His grip a vice, does not let go,
A watchful kite who circles slow
A wasp unhurried for he knows… a bite at a
  time is all he needs[17]
And as tiger fierce or the great She-bear
What monstrous acts could he then perform?

When man becomes a being from Hell
Sustaining blood from there will flow
Vindications produced to bludgeon, stun
Dry lightning leaps in blinding red
Thunder bolts aim to pierce the joints
Triggering tumult in the nerves

Goodness stunted, Evil monstrous
Broken the laws of God and Man
Old voices say a time will come
When Man will swim in the ox's mire
And scale the tops of pepper plants[18]
The Silver Cowrie is the *Thlen*

---

17 Having watched the steady, repetitious, robotic up-and-down movement of a wasp's head as it chews wood to build a nest, I appreciate the economy of Khasi as a language, for the phrase *"roit roit"* which Tham uses to describe this process is all that is needed to convey to the Khasi reader or listener the entire concept and rhythm of the wasp's single-minded attention to his task. In English however I have had to use more than two words to convey this effect.

18 Lines 4–5 in this stanza refer to the Khasi's deep belief that the only wealth which matters is that of the spirit. Any neglect or violation of this cherished belief diminishes human stature to such an extent that it is possible for a man to metaphorically swim in water-hollows created by the hoof prints of cattle, or enable him to clamber easily to the top of slender chili plants. A reliable source, Bah Khongsit (see Acknowledgements) however also informed me that his father used to grow chili pepper plants which had thick roots and sturdy stems. These were vastly different from the slender chili-pepper plants familiar to most of us. Apparently it was possible to lean against these robust plants without the plant bending under pressure.

Greed's a chasm like the *Mawïew* ravine
A depth no one can hope to fill
Yet he who endures, strives to hold on
In whom the will to good remains
To him the vision will be tendered
Of wind-stirred palms above *Mawïew* gorge

Thus as he journeys round the world
Man sinks and drowns in waters dark
His face begins to dim and darken
The rising smoke it thickens chokes
Though many a voyager may stay afloat
Far, far away let me escape!

 Listen to an audio recording of the poem at
https://doi.org/10.11647/OBP.0137.19

8. U Rngiew–The Dark One

Scenes from myth along with multiple images of terror and menace are used to describe how the twisted nature of evil wreaks moral havoc. Here is a place that is dark and forbidding where the deadening sense of miasmic heat and torpor is inescapable. Images of sick elephants tottering helplessly into murky swamps and serpents coiling around every tree add to the atmosphere of malaise and prowling treachery. Nightmares peopling the Khasi imagination are given free rein, like the pursuing "hounds released by their Mother Fear". The ruling deity and embodiment of all evil is The Dark One—*U Rngiew*—shape-shifter *par excellence* possessing the ability to lure and entrap.

The Dark One[1]

Far from the city where humans dwell
A forest grows where the Dark One lives
Here the face of the Moon is dark
Here the eyes of the owl burn bright
Eternal are the clouds that shroud
This hometown of the *Nongshohnoh*[2]

---

1   As mentioned earlier, "*U*" in Khasi is masculine and "*Ka*" is feminine. So the Dark One, a malignant being, is a "he". Usually "*rngiew*" or "*ngiew*" is associated with the sinister as in "*syrngiew*" (shadow) or "*i ngiew*" (looks or feels dark and disturbing). Interestingly however "*Ka Rngiew*", therefore feminine, has little to do with "*U Rngiew*" or that sense of "*ngiew*". See p. 38, n. 8.

2   Henchman employed by families who worship the *Thlen*—the man-eating snake. The word literally means "he who does not hesitate to strike (a blow)", once he has cornered victims whose blood is needed to placate the wealth-providing but ever-hungry Serpent Deity.

Translation and Notes © Janet Hujon, CC BY 4.0   https://doi.org/10.11647/OBP.0137.08

Here it was since Time began
That Evil came to dam a swamp
In tottered elephants seizured, sick
Darkly heaved the ponderous ooze
With kindling from Satanic Fires[3]
The prowler lights his furtive path

A squelchy mire which smoke calls home
Where toxic fumes douse glowing fires
Here one finds there's no escape
From the dragging-down oppressive heat
Indecision with her lonely face
Has feet imprisoned in the clay

Everywhere the air reeks stench
Serpents wrapped round every tree
In every chasm every gulf
Evil's jaw a trap full primed
Oh you who throng the vault of heaven… listen feel
    and wonder why
An uproar churns in Earth's dark belly

Feline offspring his face soot-black, knocks and begs
    from door to door,
Shape-shifter from the Hill of Death
A stag one moment, a tiger the next
Stampedes wild bison which scatter confused,
A goddess at times, a monster at others
The day before a strand of pearls, today a serpent's coil

Hound with flung-bone pinion in his throat
Transforms with ease to a docile lamb
His coat is soft… so tender-soft
His words beguiling gentle flow
Yet herded to the pen at dusk
Straight he streaks to the deepest cave

---

3   The "kindling" used is actually dry bamboo—"*prew*"—which burns easily and
brightly. Bamboo grows widely in the Khasi and Jaiñtia Hills and is a wonderful
natural resource with a variety of practical uses.

The *Rakot*'s bones hard limestone layers
Her blood congealed to coal,
Khyrwang-draped *U Ramshandi*,[4]
His mighty club heaves to anoint
Head over heels his victims roll
Roars the abyss in vast applause!

A black wind rises in the forest
With every breath of the Serpent King
From shadow worlds he drags down low
Ka Shritin-tin, Ka Mistidian
Along with seizure-blighted vultures
Oh what these spectres! *Ram Thakur*![5]

Meanwhile *Ka Lapubon, Lotikoina*
Sing their spells in the dead of night
Release caged torment long confined
In the prison owned by the King of Death,
Words they use to hook to bait
Nine times over Truth is twisted, turning cartwheels
    without end

---

4   Limestone and coal are minerals found in the Khasi and Jaiñtia Hills. The word
     "*Rakot*" is the Khasi corruption of "*rakshasas*" the demons of Hindu mythology who,
     as shape-shifters, can be either male or female. According to H. W. Sten in his book
     Na Ka Myndai sha Ka Lawei, Tham here illustrates the concept that evil appears in
     different guises, such as The Dark One and *U Ramshandi* (a blood-thirsty deity). As
     a sorcerer Evil works his dark magic even on heavenly beings like *Ka Shritin-tin, Ka
     Mistidian, Lapubon* and *Lotikoina* who become agents of his dark arts. See ns. 5 and 8
     below for more information.
        Khyrwang is a piece of cloth woven from *eri* silk (now also known as *ahimsa-silk*)
     worn as a shawl by men and wrapped sarong-style by women. Its distinctive stripes
     make it instantly recognisable as a traditional product of the *Ri Bhoi* District of
     Meghalaya. For more on this see https://yourstory.com/2015/07/daniel-syiem/ and
     http://www.vam.ac.uk/blog/fabric-of-india/guest-post-eri-weaving-in-meghalaya
5   *Ram Thakur* could be (1) the Hindu God *Ram*. Or (2) *Ram Thakur* who lived between
     1860 and 1949. His followers believed he was an avatar of Truth, a deity who
     appeared in human form to bring salvation to all. Given that this stanza is about
     false gods and demons, I feel Soso Tham here is not calling upon God *Ram* or *Ram
     Thakur* for help. To Tham the devout Christian and a patriotic Khasi, *Ram Thakur*
     represents a baneful threat. As S. K. Bhuyan writes in his introduction to *Ki Sngi
     Barim*, Soso Tham's "... patriotism has led him to an overwhelming bias for the
     manners and traditions of his native land".

An unblemished Name is a mighty shield
Protects the unkempt destitute[6]
"God of Truth" — "The Nine Above"
"The Words of Those Who Came Before",[7]
While God calls man to heaven above
U Rngiew drags him down to Hell's Nine Tiers

Rogue elephant *U Pablei Lawbah*,[8]
Trumpets long from forest fringes
The untouched beauty of the moon
Forever bruised and blemished since
The medium's speech a bewildering babble
Forked the tongue of this Red-Crested One

Towards him sludges the *Umsohsun*[9]
Turbid with the rush of rot
The human face tough-skinned, dull-browed
A mask for evil locked within
The red-headed god lifts to his lips
A lavish feast of toads and frogs

---

6   According to Sten, Tham is probably referring to the manipulative *Pablei Lawbah* (see footnote 8 below) who was protected by a number of eminent citizens of Khasi society who believed him to be a (Khasi) god-incarnate.

7   The words within quotation marks are supposed to be those uttered by *Pablei Lawbah* whom Soso Tham denounces as a false Messiah.

8   Again according to Sten, Tham here intertwines two stories—that of *U Dormi* called *Pablei Lawbah* by his followers, and *U Rngiew*. *U Dormi* was a cult figure who proclaimed himself the reincarnation of *U Sohpet Bneng* and was by some looked upon as a deity. Soso Tham was horrified that a mere human being should call himself a God (*Pa* means father and *blei* means God) and thus run counter to the original Khasi belief in the one and only Creator-God. So the specific details relating to *Pablei Lawbah* as being the medium through which God spoke to the people, are recounted here to explain the poet's wrath at an impostor who, as a medium, is supposed to have spoken in the voices of alien deities like *Ram Thakur* (see footnote 5 above) and (now) evil female spirits (*Ka Shritin-tin, Ka Mistidian, Ka Lapubon, Ka Lotikoina*). With his "forked tongue" he bewitched a susceptible audience. *Pablei Lawbah* is a travesty of the real Saviour—the Noble Rooster who according to Khasi belief, interceded with God. In the Christian context he was a Pretender to the throne of grace on which sits Christ the saviour. *Pablei Lawbah* is like the mythical *U Rngiew* who also adopts several guises to lure and ensnare his unsuspecting victims.

9   A locality in Shillong named after the stream *Umsohsun* (*Um* means water). Filthy waste from part of the town drains into the stream which consequently never runs pure.

The nine clear springs will soon run dry[10]
And so will haunting pools of tears
Demonic howls will rent the skies
A clamorous din will swell the earth,
When man ingests all that he can
That day will be his last on earth

Kyllang, Symper of might profound[11]
Will either drown or float away
The hardest flint of stubborn mould
Will detonate in a firestorm
The inferno consumes *Bah-Bo Bah-Kong*[12]
The Black Serpent King is drenched in red!

His peeling skin with ease sloughs off
Child of change he now can fly
Alone he circles shadowy lands
And then at last a fire-serpent
Wicked heart of toxic envy
Burns reduces all to ash

At the city-gates where The Dark One lives
Stand barking dogs bred to attack
Chants are heard, apparitions haunt, creepers hide
    malignant imps[13]

---

10   These are the nine springs on Shillong Peak from which our rivers take their being.
11   *Kyllang* is a dome of granite rising from the countryside of *Hima Nongkhlaw*, and *Symper* found in *Hima Maharam*, is a hill covered in lush forests. *Hima* means kingdom or fiefdom. *Kyllang* and *Symper* are said to have been the abode of two mountain spirits, brothers whose rivalry led to a bitter battle recounted in a legend that explains the particular physical aspect of these two hills. See Kynpham Singh Nongkynrih's *Around the Hearth: Khasi Legends*, pp. 80–83.
12   The legendary forests on the slopes of *Bah Bo Bah Kong* in Narpuh (Jaiñtia Hills) are now no more thanks to the unholy alliance between greedy politicians and cement companies. What Tham thought unimaginable in his lifetime has tragically come to pass.
13   Khasis tell tales of a will-o-the-wisp creature that lures unsuspecting travellers. One traveller managed to wound one such spirit with his arrow and, following the trail of blood left by the spirit, finally came to a dead end by a creeper where the evil sprite is said to have taken refuge.

There also thrive—fevers, pestilence perplexity plague;
The Sanctified Spirit offered to all[14]
By he now ordained—"Venerable Uncle, Respected Father"

Mindless Terror the Cavern King
Night and day He seeks out prey
In every home a pack released
Hounds unleashed by their Mother Fear
From hellish gutters come these dogs
Howling devils who roam the earth

Like the hornet, ravenous demon
U Rngiew delights in startling prey
(In the crook of her arm, secure on her hip, Death safely
    holds her child Lament)
He gorges on from dawn till dusk
Through Spring and Summer, Autumn, Winter
Day after day and night after night, helplessly caught
    in the grip of greed

Stirring flames to wild abandon
The Serpent's hiss illumes the night
From tops of boulders rough and craggy
The grey owl moans "*Kitbru, kitbru!*"[15]
Unbroken howls on snow-capped peaks
Jackals wailing without end

Many are those who hide from him
They burrow deep into their beds

---

14   Devotees of the *Thlen* are said to set aside rice beer for a year by which time
     the drink is so strong as to cloud the drinker's judgement, emboldening him to
     commit murder without a shred of regret. This is the "consecrated spirit" given
     to their henchmen—the *nongshohnoh*. Rice beer also forms part of the main Khasi
     socio-religious ceremonies (weddings, naming ceremonies, death). All these are
     conducted in places that have been blessed and designated as hallowed and sacred.
     The use of this staple ritual to further evil underlines the twisted blasphemous
     nature of *U Rngiew* and those who purportedly worship the *Thlen*.
15   In keeping with the ominous nature of night, the call of the owl—"*kitbru, kitbru*"—
     definitely carries a sinister message. *Kit* means carry away and *bru* means people.

In homes in caves in tall spared grass[16]
They sleep by day, are awake by night
Women, children fear the dark
Sinister shadows, shaggy-haired… menace prowls
    outside their doors

From deep within the midnight dark
The devil's blaze sheds fitful light
On the dancing wraith upon a *Phiang*,[17]
Kyndong-dong-dong goes the tapping drum
And when the jaws are poised to clamp
Strange markings streak the earthen pot

A windrush stoop to *Pamdaloi*[18]
From where he journeys round the world
He hovers in wait by that open door
Once inside, a vessel his haven
The life of their souls entrusted to him
Forever a king in bliss and contentment

In ancient hamlets back in time
One word echoes—"Curse!"—it calls
In those dwellings where he lives
Light struggles hard to defeat the dark
Hope takes flight, rejects, abandons,
The homes of the *Thlen*—they wither die out

---

16   The "tall spared grass" refers to swathes of grass left uncut and never cleared for cultivation or eaten by grazing animals. It is usually found on the peripheries of villages. The grass follows its own cycle of life, death and regeneration, thriving on the rich organic matter into which it breaks down. It is so lush and thick that it is said to make a comfortable bed for a tiger.

17   *Phiang* is short for "Khiewphiang", a water pot found in most Khasi homes. The "he" referred to here is the *Thlen*. It is said that when devotees bring him offerings of human blood, the victim appears as a spirit dancing to the accompaniment of drums on a silver plate, casting a shadow on the side of the water pot.

18   The name of the village where the *Thlen*'s cave is located. The verse shows how evil personified by the *Thlen* and *U Rngiew*, enters homes whose inhabitants have an intense desire for wealth. Again a reference to the legend of the *Thlen*, who was nurtured by humans who tried unsuccessfully to destroy him—a metaphor for man's endless struggle against the lure of wealth.

Red-hot spike lodged in his craw[19]
They pulled him out of his ancient cave
They chopped his body into bits, to feast on his remains,
But a morsel forgotten grew into a seed
Invasive hungry rampant wild
Spawning swarms in sites undreamt—those caverns of
    the human heart

Where pitch-black are the sun and moon
Far reaches where the wraith sheds tears
The lovely maiden a wandering recluse
Why does she roam wild-eyed alone?
The serpent's coils are tightly wrapped
Around the blooming *Amirphor*.[20]

 Listen to an audio recording of the poem at
https://doi.org/10.11647/OBP.0137.20

---

19 Another reference to the legend of the *Thlen* whose own greed ultimately caused
    his downfall. Accustomed to being fed human flesh he opened his huge mouth
    to receive more, realising too late that a red-hot stake had been hurled into his
    throat. He died in torment and it is believed that his writhing caused earthquakes
    so strong as to alter the topography of the land forever. Myths about the history of
    the land ascribe the Khasis' fold mountains to this event. See Nongkynrih, *Around
    the Hearth*, 64–72.
20 The word is probably Sanskrit or Persian in origin. "*Amar*" in Sanskrit means
    immortal and "*Amir*" in Persian is one whose soul and memory does not die.
    "(*Amir*)*phor*" would be the Khasi pronunciation of "*phol*"or "*phal*" which in Hindi
    means fruit. So perhaps this is a reference to an Immortal Fruit or Flower, which
    makes sense within the context of cultural jeopardy that so troubled Soso Tham.

9. U Simpyllieng–The Rainbow

Out of relentless darkness hope emerges and here we begin to feel the calm benediction of light. Although the rainbow as a symbol of hope is appropriate in any culture, in the rain-lashed Khasi Hills where the Monsoon exults in unleashing its power, the colours of the rainbow arcing against freshly washed skies will obviously have a special resonance. Nature and Myth both underline the constancy of hope and mercy, provided mankind repents of his sin of pride and seeks forgiveness from his God.

The Rainbow

The face of the earth polluted by sin
The God within has taken flight
"Ascent" "Descent" forever ceased[1]
A people gripped by terror fear
Blinded choked by infernal hordes
"O where is He, He whom we love"[2]

---

1   Referring to the time when the golden ladder, the "mediator" between heaven and Earth on *U Sohpet Bneng* had not been removed by God and human beings could move easily between the two domains.
2   "He" is the saviour. As Soso Tham was a devout Christian, one assumes he is referring to Christ.

Translation and Notes © Janet Hujon, CC BY 4.0   https://doi.org/10.11647/OBP.0137.09

Wisdom, Knowledge, Contemplation
Blindly stumble in the dark,
A widowed mother children held close
Cursed by memories helpless, alone.
Lost to us the *Amirphor*[3]
All that is left is the *Ekjakor*[4]

The world lies awake at the witching hour
Stars drown themselves in Hell's deep void
Throughout this black impenetrable night
Grant us relief O Morning Star
You who with the rooster's clarion
Welcomes the light that will drench the world

Crippled by affliction, crushed by illness
We glimpse the rim of earth's dark belly,[5]
As when we encounter tiger bear
Our souls recoil and shrink with fear
The ceremony of colour now faded frail
"Rites, divinations—confusion confounded!"

What then is Right and what Transgression?
Though fervent the atonement, clan numbers decline
—"For Me! For Me!" Insatiable the demons, insistent the
    clamour[6]
The dignity of sacrifice most solemn profaned
Dried is the nectar, just the comb remains[7]
"O hear us, we pray! You who made us, placed us here
    on earth!"

---

3   See p. 50, n. 20.
4   A mythical Dragon/Serpent.
5   The earth here is a grave/a tomb—although the earth is also seen as the womb of
     life.
6   Khasis believe that illness and affliction are either signs of divine or demonic
     visitations. A person's health could only be restored when the particular god or, as
     in this case demon, has been appeased.
7   Honey, especially that collected from orange groves in the Khasi Hills, is one of
     Meghalaya's most prized products. Honey is a metaphor for sweetness and plenty.

As children die
Deceived betrayed[8]
Maggot, Fly and sickly Vulture
The only clans to grow and prosper
To lift the *Shyngwiang* to their lips[9]
Conducting rituals, performing last rites

"A basket of seeds yields a mere *khoh* of grain[10]
Much you will spend, but meagre your gain
One at dawn another at night
They give up the ghost so that I might live
For that's how I'm fed, and from hunger am spared."
So sings the crow as she circles above
Those offerings of rice that are left for the dead![11]

The Midnight King ascends the throne
The world spirals down into Circles of Hell
Man wanders the world to look for a way
To rebuild restore the Covenant broken
For light to rise from deep in the dark
And for an insurgence of song to break out in his heart

Flames from the altar will rise to the skies
To Heaven man lifts his troubled gaze
When will the Dawn unveil herself?
When will the firmament blush a deep red?
And how from amongst a cohort of devils,
Will one stand upright and alone to face God?

---

8   A reference to the folktale of the ox punished by his Maker for his disobedience. See p. 35, n. 1.
9   A flute played during religious ceremonies.
10 A *khoh* is a basket with sides tapering to a point and carried on the back with the aid of a head strap. It is used to carry a variety of goods including market-produce, firewood and pots of water from a spring or communal tap.
11 As part of the funeral rites, offerings of rice are left for the deceased at cremation sites, thus providing food for the crow, the bird who for personal gain persuades the ox to lie to mankind. See p. 35, n. 1.

One who strives to seek and appraise
Comprehending the mystery of divinations and rituals
Who evaluates, debates to challenge his Maker:
"Freely, generously, give of your blessings!"
He will plead for himself, stand up for his clan
To wrest divine pardon for sins and transgressions

"To shoulder sin, to bear the yoke
  Make strong *Ka Rngiew*, to cleanse the curse",[12]
These the words of God our King
Heard at the Durbar of Thirty Beasts,[13]
"Until the Prince of Song arrives[14]
Who consents to bear pain to save mankind?"

So spoke our God our Lord above
What answer will the Durbar give
In silence long the hushed world sat
Eyelids drooped beasts fell asleep
One question lingering on the lips of man
"The Prince of Song, when will he sing?"[15]

---

12   See p. 38, n. 8.
13   Thirty is a number Khasis use to indicate a great many.
14   *Simpah/Simkaro* is the name given to a gifted Intercessor. *Sim* means bird, *pah* means
     song or singing. I have translated the word into "Prince of Song" but to fully
     understand what "Song" means, it is important to remember that, among Khasis,
     songs are outpourings which have their root in religious observances. See n. 15
     below.
15   *Sim-karo* (like *Simpah*): this term is a metaphor for a man elected as leader
     for his altruistic and trustworthy qualities. He is seen as the agent of light and
     transformation as willed by God.
        According to Sten (p. 77), Khasis see the root of their creativity in their outpourings
     of prayer and thanksgiving to God. It is through these acts of worship that Khasis
     express their understanding of their place in this world and their relation to God.
     Thus poetry is linked to the sacred and the divine, and the poet is in many ways
     God's agent whose song draws those who suffer under the yoke of sin back to the
     divine.

Stop! Now listen from *Ka Krem Lamet Ka Krem Latang*[16]
Keeper of his Word, the Rooster speaks:[17]
"Until the day of the Awaited One
Come what may I will bear the burden
To spare mankind eternal woe
When before his Creator God he stands."

Thus he addressed the assembled Durbar
Fearless he stood holding fast to his word
Crossing the threshold of the Sun's domain
He claps his hands and she wakes from sleep
And when the rooster thrice had crowed
The earth once more was bathed in light

The land, the soil began to bloom
Trust returned fear exorcised
Foreboding sank in *Ka Diengïei*[18]
Along with her demonic troops
Vivid all auguries, signs and predictions
Divinations and reckonings deciphered made clear

A shroud now lifted from the face of man
Who once again "ascends" "descends"
Heaven and Earth united as one
For man stands upright to appease his God
Peace shall reign throughout the land
Visible once more the King of the Skies[19]

---

16   The Cave into which the Sun retreated in anger, depriving mankind of light. See Chapter 3, pp. 21–22.
17   Again refers to the same legend of the Rooster offering himself as a sacrifice to the Sun so that she would forgive mankind and restore light to the world.
18   The monstrous tree that plunged the world into darkness (see Chapter 3, pp. 20–21).
19   "King of the Skies" refers to either the rainbow or Christ. Based on the words ascribed to the rooster in verse 13 ("Until the day of the Awaited One/I'll bear the burden come what may…"), Sten maintains that Soso Tham saw Christianity as the final flowering of the indigenous Khasi belief in a saviour releasing the world from the darkness of sin. See Sten, *Na Ka Myndai*, p. 79. The underlying belief of both faiths is hope and salvation through a "mediator".

Gleam of sky on rock we'll see
When sun-showers stop and fade away
Dense dark clouds in fear retreat
When the Rainbow rises in the sky
When man grinds Satan underfoot
He then becomes a Child of God

When long ago the earth was pure
Dark was both the Sun and Moon
But through the dense relentless night
The Star of Hope refused to die
The Gift of Mercy man receives
When before his God he bends his knee.

Listen to an audio recording of the poem at
https://doi.org/10.11647/OBP.0137.21

10. *Ka Ïing I Mei*–Home

A more literal translation of the title is "The House that Belongs to my Mother" or "My Mother's Home". Here "Mei" refers both to the biological mother *and* to the poet's homeland, for both have nurtured the poet's being. With the dawn of hope and light in the preceding section it is natural that the poet now describes what it feels like to be home. He goes back in time to his childhood and to the daily rituals where the sacred codes of life are affirmed. Finally, he moves on to describe the rituals of death with reference to the concluding lines of *Ki Sngi Barim*, where the poet talks of arriving at the House of God—the everlasting mother of all homes and sanctuaries. But what is always characteristic and remarkable about Soso Tham is that his presentation of the most weighty and serious of subjects is endowed with an inescapable energy. Since for Soso Tham his culture is so obviously *alive*, he cannot but describe it in dynamic and vivid terms. Even the rendition of ceremonies for the dead is undeniably joyful.

When a Khasi man marries he leaves the house where he was born—the home of his clan—and moves into his wife's house—the home of *her* clan which is referred to as *"ka ïing khun"* (his children's home)—to differentiate it from *"ka ïing kmie"*—his mother's home. These expressions seem to suggest that in both cases it is never *his* home, pointing to the limbo-land the Khasi man inhabits. But others have countered this by saying that both as father (progenitor) and maternal uncle (protector and adviser) a man has a significant place in the family. This is true if theory and practice concur and if traditional reverence for the role of the uncle remains unchanged. But it would be foolish

Translation and Notes © Janet Hujon, CC BY 4.0   https://doi.org/10.11647/OBP.0137.10

to disregard the complexities of life on the ground. The advent of the nuclear family, the need to seek a living away and often far from the traditional hearth combined with the increased obeisance paid to wealth as the only criterion for respect, are factors eroding this way of thinking and the role of protector and advisor traditionally associated with the figure of the uncle will depend on the persistence of such values. Some men in the community have voiced their discontent, feeling that the uncle/father has responsibilities but no real power in a society where women inherit property and have tangible material assets, and where children's identity is defined by the mother's clan. Feminists counter this argument by pointing out that only well-off women can claim to be landowners, and that to this day women are not allowed an equal voice in the decision-making process of traditional organisations—they are still denied access to the public sphere. The controversy simmers.

Home[1]

Let me return to the field we tended, the field we owned,
Back to that world dreamed up by tears,
As does the deer at the end of her days
When weary, spent and faint with wandering
She retraces paths that once she trod.
O once again to be home with *Mei*!

---

1   The phrase "*Ka ïing i Mei*" can be literally translated into "My Mother's House" or "The House which belongs to my Mother", but neither convey the many layered meanings *experienced* by the Khasi speaker. Used as a prefix when addressing a person, the honorific "*i*" connotes a combination of love and respect which shades into reverence, and when "*i*" accompanies the word "*Mei*" (mother), a figure central to the network of family relationships in matrilineal Khasi society, the profound sense of homage and love the child tenders the mother is deepened and consequently immeasurable. So "My Mother's Home or House" fails to convey that *felt* sense of love and near-worship. As a Khasi, I feel a sense of poignancy when the married son speaks these words for he is looking back at the birth-home he has left behind. In relation to this I have also tried to recall whether daughters ever say "*ngan leit sha ïing i Mei*" ("I will go to my mother's house") with that same sense of absolute separation as is detected when a man makes the same statement. I do not think so. Given that this section of the narrative describes Khasi customs, "*ïing*" also has a more general application referring to the Motherland of the Khasis (The "i" in "*i Mei*" is pronounced as the "i" in Spanish or Italian).

There as a boy I set my first traps
There the owl called out at night
Gone the birds that soared from the gorge
And where the *Skong*, the *Lapohiat*?[2]
Breathless winds cool on the skin, waters with the bite of ice
Today I find them still and quiet, listening in the lonely silence

"San ka Kong Ri, pat ka Kong A"[3]
We chanted as siblings whenever we played
Young and tender the Sun and Moon
In that far-off time where I learnt to sing
Where once we were whole not broken and scattered
In that faraway place we first learnt to know God

The *Wahkaba* roars as she has always done
The *Latara* leaps with her customary joy[4]
The child in us is never lost
Lives on in the adult we grow to become
So I stand as before on the lip of the gorge
Then tell me why my blood runs cold?

A time we felt and thought as one
Sweet the call—*"Meisan, Meinah"*
We stepped out then, one clan, one womb[5]

---

2   *Skong—Chimonobambusa callosa*: a type of bamboo used as posts in the construction of houses. *Lapohiat—Ligustrum lucidum*, a wild fruit-bearing tree providing food for birds.

3   In her desperate attempts to escape the clutches of an evil Tiger and a tyrannical Toad, Nam—the heroine of one of the best-known Khasi legends—chants these magic words. Seeking the help of the cotton and rubber trees (*Kya* and *Jri—Bombax ceiba/Bombax malabaricum* and *Ficus Elastica*) she asks them to grow (*san*) then wait (*pat*) at a pace in tune with the rhythm of her efforts to reach the safe haven of the "Moon, the Stars and the Sun" far from the dark kingdom of menace ruled by the Tiger and Toad. See Nongkynrih's *Around the Hearth*: "Ka Nam and the Tiger", p. 49.

4   Waterfalls in the Khasi Hills.

5   Among the Khasis all sisters of the mother are regarded as potential "mothers" (hence the prefix "*Mei*") and when a female sibling dies often one of the sisters takes care of the orphaned nieces or nephews. Hence the mother's older sister is referred to as the older mother (*Mei* means mother, *san* older/mature); the mother's younger sister is the younger or the girl-like mother (*nah* is short for *khynnah*, a word used to refer to children, to someone who is young, innocent and relatively inexperienced); the mother's sisters all hail from the same clan, are descended from the same ancestral mother and therefore of the "same womb".

Birds of one colour flocking together
Gathering to roost in the home of the *khatduh*[6]
This is and has been the life of the clan

In their grass-thatched homes the *Hynñiew Trep*
Held up a flare of blazing conviction
Proclaiming as they did with one strong voice
"For our numbers to increase, for our own to prosper"
Then as with bees in creviced rock
Tenderly the mother caresses, holds close

All noble kings from distant lands
Seek the house where concord dwells
A kingdom honouring "kith and kin"
A land where is found "the Uncle, the Father"[7]
And where can be found the Ancestral Mother?[8]
Her seat at the centre, the heart of the hearth

Where from days of old, days lost to us
The wealth of clan and race took root

---

6   "*Khatduh*": youngest daughter—the custodian of family rites and rituals and responsible for their continued practice.

7   *U Kur U Kha* ("kith and kin")—One of the most sacred tenets of Khasi society is to know (*tip*) the members of your own clan—your *kur*—and also those of your father's—your *kha*. This is to ensure that the most horrific of taboos is never violated—entering into a sexual relationship with members of your own clan. According respect to the members of your father's clan is another sacred obligation, for without the father a child does not come into being, is never born. The root of the word *kha* relates to the act of birth.
       To try and communicate the many-layered meaning of the original word "*don*" (in the third line), I have used the word "found". The literal meaning of "*don*" is "to have/has" in the sense of "have got" which I feel does not convey the wider cultural significance which also includes bestowed respect and which is in turn linked to self-respect. Having or being seen to have a Maternal Uncle and a Father, those traditional givers of invaluable advice and support, is a matter of family and clan pride. I hope the word *found* implies not only that a family knows for certain that it *has* guardians and mentors, but also suggests that the outsider, in this case the "noble king" can "*find*" or see for themselves how culturally blessed that kind of family is.

8   As Khasis are a matrilineal society the Ancestral Mother of each clan (*Ka Mei, Ka Ïaw*) is a being who occupies a venerated space in the psyche of all Khasis, as is the maternal uncle (*U Kñi*). The hearth is the centre of the traditional Khasi home.

Where liturgies were honed, incantations intoned
And our native Creed sprang into life
A smouldering fire of enduring force
Inspiring a thirst to establish new worlds

Like deer *serow* we were surefooted once
Over limestone rock and precipice sheer
Purses were woven for hunters of *sbai*[9]
Who were ready and poised at the first thrust of light
Concern for the living, respect for the dead[10]
Those touchstones of "greatness a clan can achieve"

Thus declared the Uncles the Ancients
Their words the Law within each clan
In ceremonies of colour, at celebratory pageants
Or when turbulent wars shuddered the land
Gathered the "Nine who shoulder the bow"
Quivers the sword, dances the Shield

The role of the son is to defend
His home, his clan, ancestral lands[11]
The family wealth the daughter safeguards
Tending the herds of cattle and goats
For a tree to bear fruit what name shall it bear?
So followed the rite to pour and anoint[12]

---

9   Cowries were once used as currency.

10 These principles are described in the next section, *Ka Meirilung* (Gentle Motherland).

11 Khasi thanksgiving dances symbolically reflect this custom when male dancers move in a circle around the women attired in traditional finery of silk and gold, not to parade wealth but to display God's blessings for which the people are thankful.

12 Khasis believe that a person's health and well-being ("for the tree to bear fruit") depends on the right choice of name which is decided upon in a ceremony where a priest prays and then calls out, one by one, the names chosen by the family and as he does so pours from a gourd containing a suspension of ground rice and water. It is only when this mixture of rice and water holds together in a small drop that clings to the mouth of the gourd, that the name spoken at the time is chosen to be the one favoured by God. The child is then marked or anointed with the rice-water and so are the families of the father and mother. For a description and detailed analysis of the Khasi Naming Ceremony, see Bijoya Sawian, *et al.*, *The Main Ceremonies of the Khasi* (Guwahati: Vivekananda Kendra Institute of Culture, 2012), chapter I, pp. 1–6.

Pay heed to your forebears, your *Kur*, your *Kha*[13]
They have read the signs, know what perils await
Taboo and danger they observe they respect
For lightning smites, the tiger bites
He who scorns taboo is the devil's apprentice
Head shaven in furrows, branded with shame, relentlessly
    hounded, forever exiled

A sword and shield in every home
Close at hand, companions in sleep
To safeguard family, clan and race
Rises the sword, the spear, the shield
So sparing our children a beggar's existence
Flesh of our flesh, blood of our blood

Bones laid to rest in the Great Ossuary[14]
An accompaniment of drums escorting them there
Pillars of stone for women and men
Memorials erected once oblations are offered,
Out in the open in passionate abandon
Dazzling the dance of silk and brocade, joined even by gold
    habitually discreet,[15]

Distinct the clans of the mother and father
Reverential the homage to ancestors long gone[16]
On burial hills *"Meisan Meinah"*[17]
Side-by-side they will always sleep

---

13 See p. 60, n. 7.
14 Khasis who hold onto the indigenous faith cremate their dead, after which the bones of the departed are finally laid to rest in a Great Ossuary which is the afterlife sanctuary on earth for all the members of one clan.
15 This verse shows how ceremonies for the dead are festive occasions in which the living honour the dead and "celebrate" their lives. Homage to the dead is paid in music and colour while stone memorials are powerful long-living symbols of remembrance—all, as it were, is set in stone.
16 See p. 60, n. 7. Certain rites observed during the ceremony conducted for the dead clearly demonstrate that even in death Khasis continue to foreground the sacrosanct pre-eminence of that most significant of all knowledge—knowing your kith and kin, so that the most heinous of all taboos of marrying into one's clan is never broken.
17 The older mother, the younger mother. See p. 59, n. 5.

Journeying together to the House of God
United as one even in death

Thunders the dark in an uproar of colour
When a nobleman's son is laid on his pyre
Concourse resplendent in *Dhara* and *Ryndia*[18]
Ornaments worn of coral and gold
And when handsome young men begin moving in dance
Tears drop from the eyes of young maidens who watch.

 Listen to an audio recording of the poem at
https://doi.org/10.11647/OBP.0137.22

---

18 The *Ryndia* and *Dhara* are part of Khasi traditional apparel. The former is normally
worn by men like a shawl, a turban, or draped round the neck to hang from the
shoulders like a scarf. The *Dhara* is usually associated with women and is draped
Grecian fashion but over both shoulders. However, sometimes on ceremonial
occasions men wear it as a *dhoti*.

11. *Ka Meirilung–*
Gentle Motherland

In the plaintive lyrical opening of this section Soso Tham asks that most human of questions—Where do we come from? For the Khasi the answer still lies in conjecture. Meanwhile they suffer the humiliation of forced identities which are at best perplexing, and at worst humiliating. It is from these that Tham steers us gently away. Once again he sees the natural world as a source from which to draw upon for moral strength. He lists the forethought and ingenuity of those who led before—"Dimly they glimmer, one or two", he describes the codes of warfare, and most importantly he names the luminaries who fought with pride and integrity. It is in the last verse that Tham highlights what is or should be the lasting legacy of our forebears, a principle which we would be foolish to ignore: "Boundaries defined, rights respected… Welfare and woe of common concern"—a message relevant to a troubled world.

Gentle Motherland

Tell me children of the breaking dawn
Mother-kite, mother-crow,
You who circle round the world
Where the soil from which we sprang?
For if I could, like you I'd drift
Down the ends of twelve-year roads!

O Wind who lifts those seeds of Pine
Where grows that ancient rugged Tree?

https://doi.org/10.11647/OBP.0137.11

Migrant from a Land of Plenty[1]
Perhaps that same That Faraway Land?
Or did our infant homeland crawl
From the lair of tiger *khung*[2]

So that like them our blood will course
Beating red in tendon vein
(Where Silver Strings stir into life
And I can pluck the *Duitara*)
But as we have such hardy souls
Home must have been a den of bears

The pine who grows from wind-borne seeds
Drifting in from alien lands
Though oftentimes consumed by fire
His crown is spared, remains un-scorched
His roots hold firm beneath the rock
No storm can do its wrenching worst!

In other ways once more we'll climb
With other races mingle meet
Though cast as followers, why should we fear
Have not others led before?
Vivid the signs they left behind
Resin-rich the ancient pine

On hills and in forests
Our ancients thought deeply
The *Tangmuri* sang
The *Sharati* wept[3]
Standing Stones sprang throughout the land
To remember forever "*U Kñi, U Kpa*"[4]

For the sun-beaten traveller weary and spent
Boulders were hewn into seats of rest

---

1   The original phrase (*Ri u Soh u Pai*) translates into "Land of fruit and sugarcane". I
    have chosen to use "Land of Plenty" to maintain the regularity of the rhythm, and
    also because the expression "Land of fruit and sugarcane" is often used to indicate
    abundance.
2   A mythical beast, half-lion half-bear.
3   The *Tangmuri* and *Sharati* are traditional wind instruments.
4   The Uncle, the Father.

And bridges spanned rivers linking far banks,
As long as the sun and moon remain
Forever endures *Ka Thadlaskein*[5]
Genius and strength of our ancient ones

Today in your waters O *Thadlaskein*
Only waterfowl swim and splash with joy
But in my dreams at night I see
Orchards and gardens encircling your banks
When such a Host has gone before
We can never be infants left far behind

In *Jaiñtiapur* mansions built to last
Water tanks sunk throughout the land
Signposting a future that is only envisioned
By an eye that is clear, an ear that can hear
If our homeland today is to scale great heights
Then like once they were, so should we be

"Tigers of the Sword", "Noble Bearers of Honour"
Toughened by trials through Fire and Water
Their pageantry and colour, their bearing, their pride
To behold their demeanour was to fall back in awe
Revered Ancestress, Creator Father
Will you tell us where they fell asleep?

Their name and their fame
Not mere legend or tale
U Puhshilum, U Khwai Shynreh[6]
Was untold wealth their only concern?
Was all, you think, just swallowed whole
When we grappled and battled with the rage of the
    river?[7]

---

5   *Ka Thadlaskeiñ* is a lake in the Jaiñtia Hills. Not wishing to shed the innocent blood
    of his own people by declaring war on his own king, the ruler of *Jaiñtiapur, Sajar
    Nangli* chose exile. But before leaving their homeland he and his band of rebel
    warriors used the ends of their bows to dig this lake.

6   Legendary characters famed for their superhuman strength. *U Puhshilum* was one
    who could turn over a whole hill with one thrust of his spade; *U Khwai Shynreh* used
    buffaloes as fish-bait.

7   A reference to the legend which explains how the Khasis lost their script during a
    great flood. See p. 24, n. 4.

Just one or two stars in heaven appear
One or two names remembered, survive
Sajar Laskor, Mailong Raja,
U Mangkathiang, U Syiem Kongka,[8]
Dimly they glimmer one or two
"Lest we forget! Lest we forget!"[9]

Kings they were of fearsome mien
Of them why should we be ashamed
They were not mere "Collectors of Heads"
But "Children of the Sword and Shield"
If ever we forget that they once lived
As orphans we doom ourselves to live

From under cover of cotton and rubber[10]
The resolute call to war rang out
Protectress of the Portal, Guardian Divine
Had kept tireless watch both day and night
With one accord the Tigers arose
The sword she lies still, but if war is to cease
The man in the sword must be unsheathed[11]

Swift they sped through forests deep
The tiger cowered, the *Thlen* retreats
Though slashed and torn by lightning sabres
Their sleep at night always quiet sound
Because they died to live again
Beings such as they can never age!

---

8   The names of Khasi chieftains.
9   Soso Tham was familiar with Kipling's *Recessional* and his use of this line is deeply
     ironic as we know the poet's pride in the achievements of his people, "those lesser
     breeds without the Law."
10   Cotton and rubber trees. See p. 59, n. 3 for a reference to a legend in which these
     trees play a part.
11   Translating part of this sentence "*Shynrang ka Wait*" was problematic for the original
     implies that the Sword ("*Ka Wait*"), which is female, as denoted by "*ka*", has to
     become a man—"*shynrang*". As the sword is genderless in English I have had to
     add "The sword she lies still" in order to communicate the change from female to
     male.

And so came forth these fabled warriors
Sword against sword come victory or loss
Thus ended combats of long ago
Thus did two kingdoms reconcile
"Collectors of Heads" of them you say?
Are they not "Sons of Sword and Shield"?

Oft we search for gold that's pure
Yet here we find a gold that's rare
From times now gone and times now lost
God chose those who could endure
To safeguard the frontiers of this our land
"Drenched in the blood of *U Kñi U Kpa*"

Once again will forests roar
And stones long still shake to the core
Days new unknown will surely dawn
And our homeland ripen as never before
If we are willing to listen to ponder upon
The words that are spoken by *Ka Mei Ramew*[12]

Once Great Minds did wrestle with thought
To strengthen the will, to toughen the nerve
Once too in parables they spoke they taught
In public durbar or round the family hearth
In search of a king, a being in whom
The hopes of all souls could blossom and fruit

Together as one in a circle they gathered
Learning to steer the affairs of the state
They founded a *"Hima"*[13]
Which they vowed to protect
They laid down their lives soaked the land with
their blood
Thus lives on their name, enduring their fame

---

12 Mother Earth.
13 A kingdom.

It matters not greatly who wears the crown
Only the power to shackle belongs to the king
Rich and poor, privileged and lowly
Marigold petals arranged in a circle
Resplendent gathering ordered decorous
Smoothly flow Durbar proceedings

Gateways and highways under the king's control
Tethering thongs he holds in his hands,
Though given the power to tax and to fine
No tax from land flows into his coffers
For land is common, land bequeathed
The subjects, you see, are the lords of the land[14]

Boundaries defined, rights respected
Trespass a taboo remaining unbroken
Equal all trade, fairness maintained
Comings and goings in sympathy in step
Welfare and woe of common concern
Concord's dominion on the face of the earth.

 Listen to an audio recording of the poem at
https://doi.org/10.11647/OBP.0137.23

---

14 The concept of community land ("*Ri Raid*"—common land) was once enshrined in
    Khasi traditional Law to ensure that the poor never remained landless and always
    had the means of producing their own food. Sadly this idea of "*Ri Raid*" is fast
    becoming a myth and land has now been bought and sold for private use. This is
    reminiscent of the Acts of Enclosure (1809–1820) the consequences of which tore
    apart the soul of the English poet John Clare.

12. *Lum Lamare*–Lamare Peak

This section is a dreamlike meandering through memory, myth, reflection and the immediacy of experience found in the simple pleasures of daily life. It is an account alive with movement marked by telling image and detail. Tham *names* flowers, waterfalls and rivers not only because he delights in them or because of the stories they tell, but to also underline the imaginative rapport that exists between the people and the wonders gracing their land, all of which make him finally pose the question "Which gods have made your slopes their home?"

Lamare Peak

O land of mine! When will the high Himalaya
Turn their gaze away from you?
Wind which moves to cool the hills
Will your freshness ever fade?
Yet looking back as here I stand
Was it all a passing dream?

Slow from you the flight of darkness
Well-watered tender grows your face
Orange glow in ripening groves[1]
Your granaries brim with gathered grain
Perchance in time I then can dream
Of flowering gardens everywhere

---

1   The glow of both ripe orange and betel nut.

Translation and Notes © Janet Hujon, CC BY 4.0   https://doi.org/10.11647/OBP.0137.12

The land forever tilled and living
They toil from dawn till dusk drifts in
Seeds dropped by chance unnoticed scattered
Nurture raise O Mother Earth.
Plants wild with zest our people eat
Unrivalled the taste of *Ja* on the hills[2]

Did they ever know cold? Did they ever feel heat?
Were there any tomorrows? Did night ever exist?
With burdens braced, swift, swift they raced
The whistling soared as the head strap pressed[3]
With firm support from joints robust
Thus seldom work was left undone

Girth of trees first measured then felled[4]
"Slaves from the lowlands" brought in to work[5]
Groves of maturing *kwai* and fruit
Flocks on hillsides multiplied
Clean fresh skies above a land
Where baskets brimmed, were ranged in rows

Betel-nut split on knee-caps hard[6]
Sohriew soaked, simmered and strained[7]
Milk was shunned, butter unknown

---

2   *Ja* is rice in its cooked form. So important a staple is rice in Khasi culture that the
     word for a meal is simply "*Ja*". To have a meal, whatever the accompaniments, is
     to "eat *ja*" — "*bam ja*". A meal without *ja*, no matter how nutritious and filing, is not
     worthy of the name! And the deliciousness of "*Ja* on the hills" ("*Ja ha lum*") — a meal
     eaten out in the fresh hill air — is truly a pleasure that must be tried. Soso Tham is of
     course specifically referring to simple rural delights.
3   This head strap is called *u star* — also mentioned a few lines further down below —
     and it is used in conjunction with a tapering basket called a *khoh* carried on the back
     (see p. 53, n. 10).
4   Like many indigenous peoples Khasis once worked *with* the land. Only trees of a
     certain girth were felled — i.e. those whose trunks could be encircled by the entire
     length of a head strap (*star*) without any evidence of slack. Alas today that is no
     longer the case. Commercial gain is now the sole consideration.
5   Khasis were able to hire people from lands beyond their own kingdoms — most
     probably the plains of present-day Bangladesh.
6   This is not a tall story. I have seen this done — knowing how hard a betel nut is,
     splitting it on the knee cap indicates that the bone used as a "chopping board" is
     rock-hard.
7   "Job's tears": *Coix-lachryma jobi* — belonging to the family of Grasses.

Their choice a broth of boiled beef bones
Supple-limbed, movement lithe
Deserving of ease upon a *prah*[8]

Ka knup, ka khoh, u star they wove[9]
(In forge of stone they smelted iron
Furnace-tempered knife sword axe
Fine-tipped tweezers for the offending barb)
They wandered by rivers to drink the wind
Placing baskets and snares to net a catch

United they were, agreement prevailed
(Unbroken respect for *U Kñi* and *U Kpa*)
Those were the days when maidens and men
Ploughed, sowed, weeded, hoed
So tell me then O *Lum Rapleng*[10]
Did Heaven have borders and where did they end!

Over hillside and forest profusion abounds
Vast the array of names they bestowed
U Tiew Japang on sheer cliff sides[11]
On river banks *U Tiew Tyrkhang*[12]
The light of genius now all but snuffed
Today who would know *U Tiew Khmat Miaw*?[13]

---

8   A *prah* is a round flat woven tray usually used for winnowing grain. Wheelchairs are relatively new to the region and the old, infirm and immobile were lowered onto a *prah* on which they sat either indoors or out in the warm sunshine. My great-grandmother lived so long that she reigned in state over her family in this manner. To live a long life is an achievement and the old are respected and cared for accordingly.

9   The *knup* is the Khasi farmer's rainshield and is made of palm leaves stretched and held in shape by a framework of bamboo cane strips. When viewed on the wearer's back its shape is, appropriately enough, reminiscent of a shield beetle. The *knup* protects the head and body and leaves both hands free to carry out all the tasks in the field. There is also a smaller *knup* which functions as a parasol during hot sunny days.

10   *Rapleng* Peak lies east of a village called *Nongkrem* in the Khasi Hills but is clearly visible from the Jaiñtia Hills where Soso Tham worked as a teacher.

11   *Primula denticulata.*

12   Khasi Ferns: *Dryopteris filix, Osmunda regalis.* Ferns are referred to as flowers (*tiew*) because of their subtle perfume.

13   "Flower with the face of a cat" —an orchid: *Dendrobium chrysanthum.*

Birdsong rises from the thicket
Moans the bee within his hive
The *Jalyeit* sings inside his cage[14]
While flowers in their gardens bloom
When *U Tiew Lyngskaw* is with turban crowned[15]
We gaze and gaze till all longing is spent

Their bowstrings drawn archers dance in a circle
Quiet the eye trained true on the target, steady the
    hand that rests on the ear,
On that soaring spray of black and white
On the *Sohpdung* or the wagers at stake,[16]
Couplets are chanted in mockery playful,
The ceremony of banter declares its intent

Under skies with a dusting of puffed-rice-clouds[17]
Applause breaks out again and again
When victory is won by a village entire
They dance in a circle on the Great Market Hill[18]
Back in those days which forever belong
To Sohra's young women and Sohra's young men

Soil-soaked stained throughout the day
At night they rest on beds of skin[19]
Days in the forest setting dogs on the scent

---

14 *Golden fronted chloropsis.* A songbird par excellence, able to imitate the songs of
     other birds.
15 An orchid: *Dendrobium densiflorum.*
16 The two rival teams were identified by the colour of their arrow-feathers, which
     were either black or white. *Sohpdung*—the big tubercular root of a certain plant
     used as a target during archery matches.
17 A scattering of small cumulus clouds. This expression comes from the sight of
     puffed rice (i.e. boiled rice mixed with yeast to make rice wine) scattered on the
     floor after the cat has knocked the pot over.
18 Markets in the Khasi Hills were places where people from surrounding areas
     converged to buy and sell and were held in different villages on different days
     of the week. The Great Market at Sohra (former Cherrapunjee) was one of the
     better-known.
19 The skins were usually made of cow hide.

Nights spent courting away from home
Mindful to leave by the first cockcrow
Not a moment is wasted as they tear away home

At break of day they descend to *Riwar*[20]
At nightfall sweat wiped clean away
By day they follow the honeybee
Convivial the nights made light with their banter
Unending the splutter of pot-roasted maize
Unforgettable the taste of honey-spread yam

O Moon who blooms for fourteen nights
O Night whose arms hold safe the stars,
The owl alights upon a branch
U Nongshohnoh — he lurks close by[21]
But under a sheet of coarse cotton or silk
The tired rest easy round a slow-burning fire

Varied the tales that they then told
Some raised laughter, others tears
Ki Moin Manik, Ki Lar Morti[22]
Lent their brilliance to another time
To a place some called "a savage forest"
A home to monkey langur wild!

And so they told in fable tale
Of heroes and their immortal fame
Of gardens in bloom, orchards with fruit
Lands where people lived in peace
How a pure and righteous Age
Secures accord for one and all

---

20 *Riwar*: the land of a distinct group of Khasis who call themselves *Wars* or *War Jaiñtia*.
    It resides in the region south of the Jaiñtia Hills.
21 See p. 43, n. 2. The *nongshohnoh* is the henchman of families who worship the
    man-eating serpent, the *Thlen*.
22 Precious stones.

Kynting-ting-ting through the quiet night
The *Marynthing* goads the tiger to dance
Laughter joy piping strumming
Together beneath a smoke-shafted roof
Kynting-ting-ting until the dawn
Vivid pathways of colour to enchantment beyond

U Tiew Japang with turban brocade
Captured by kings to wed royal daughters,[23]
Fish, Palm, Turtle, Egg
Leitmotifs familiar from ancient chants
Ka Mawtyngkong, Ka Wahrisa[24]
Poised they pose at the head of the gorge

The Lynx slings Thunder's sabre across his chest[25]
Ka Lalyngngi still combs her hair on precipitous cliffs[26]
Ka Syntuksiar drapes herself in silk[27]

---

23   This refers to a practice in the past, commemorated in a folktale, when young men
from the plains were taken captive by Khasi rulers as husbands for their daughters.

24   Waterfalls east of Sohra. Their names are evocative—[the waterfall at] "the stony
threshold" and "the river's applause".

25   Jealous of the Lynx's ability to wield his silver sword during a dance, the Thunder
God (*U Pyrthat*) asked to borrow the weapon, saying he wished to try the same
moves himself. The Lynx happily handed the sword over and the God immediately
leapt into the sky leaving the Lynx without his prized sword. The flashes of
lightning seen when thunder rumbles during a storm come from the Thunder
God brandishing the sword he stole from the Lynx. The Lynx's habit of leaving his
droppings in a mound is supposed to be his attempt to build a mountain that will
enable him to climb to heaven and retrieve his beloved sword.

26   *Hedychium gardnerianum*. A Khasi legend tells the story of *Ka Lalyngngi*, a beautiful
maiden who arrived late for The Dance of the Flowers because she spent far too
long getting herself ready. Filled with shame that all her efforts to be the belle of
the ball had been in vain, she flung herself off a cliff hoping she would die at the
bottom of the gorge. But she was stranded midway and transformed into a flower
that now bears her name.

27   *Syntuksiar* means the golden flower (of the Jaiñtia Hills) referencing the golden
paddy fields along the Myntdu river valley.

Ka Umngot will snatch victory from her sister[28]
Now tell us then *Bah-Bo-Bah-Kong*[29]
Which gods have made *your* slopes their home?

 Listen to an audio recording of the poem at
https://doi.org/10.11647/OBP.0137.24

---

28 *Ka Umngot* is a river that rises in the Khasi hills and ends her journey in the plains
of Bangladesh. The meandering course of the *Umngot* gave rise to a legend centring
on a race between two sisters. Though infinitely more powerful, the older sister—
Ka Iam—loses. Puffed with conceit *Ka Iam* had taken her time to start and found that
her hard-working sister (*Ka Umngot*) had long reached the finishing line.

29 The legendary forests in *Narpuh*, Jaiñtia Hills. See p. 47, n. 12.

Living root bridges of Nongriat village in East Khasi Hills district (2014). Photo by PJeganathan, CC BY-SA 4.0, https://commons.wikimedia.org/wiki/File:Living_root_bridges_of_Nongriat_village_in_East_Khasi_Hills_district,_Meghalaya_JEG7363.jpg

13. *Ka Aïom Ksiar*–Season of Gold

Should one wish to compare *Ki Sngi Barim U Hynñiew Trep* to a musical form, the polyphonic fugue would perhaps be its closest relative. In keeping with the poet's own longings and ultimate hope for a new world, it is the soaring melody of hope that is sustained throughout. At the same time Soso Tham's understanding of the frailty of human nature repeatedly introduces passages of anger, hopelessness and sombre reflection. The presence of these varied themes consequently preempts a positive finale. Soso Tham understands that the eternal lesson which Life and Nature hold for us is that the battle between light and darkness, hope and despair, life and death will always be fought—and we can either be worthy combatants or sidle down the path of least resistance.

Soso Tham wrote *Ki Sngi Barim U Hynñiew Trep* for his people and this exposition has been and will always be the poet speaking, exhorting and even pleading with his people. Nowhere is this made more clear than in the closing verses. He harks back to the shared myth of inherited beginnings and legends, to the presence of hope and joy and to the two moral pillars supporting the fabric of Khasi society—Truth and Justice. His pride in his homeland never wanes, but apprehension and doubt are never silenced. That which he has tried to reclaim and rebuild is still under threat: "Uncertain the journey of our people, our land".

However, his own belief in the homeland that has long cradled him, and the messages of renewal evident in Nature, reassert their force and thus reawaken hope and optimism. He ends with a collective prayer of thanksgiving, a renewing of vows and a vision of joyous abandon before making a natural transition to the end of his own earthly journey

Translation and Notes © Janet Hujon, CC BY 4.0   https://doi.org/10.11647/OBP.0137.13

and his arrival in the House of God where he will first seek out his beloved mother—*i Mei*—the acknowledged heart beating at the centre of the Khasi world. It is only appropriate that, after this man's long journey in search of the resurrection and of enlightenment transcending time and doubt, that he should finally look for the one being to whom he owes the breath of life, to whom he was once joined by a life-giving cord—his mother. This is the quiet end towards which *Ki Sngi Barim U Hynñiew Trep* moves. The poet's quest has come full circle—in his end is his beginning.

Season Of Gold

> When in midnight black the land was wrapped
> Truth was slow to reveal herself
> Seven springs then journeyed down
> From their waters man could drink
> Slow slow the flooding of the light
> As the Name of God was revealed to us
>
> From among the *Sixteen* who dwelt above
> *Seven* came to live below
> To reveal the light of Holy Truths
> Obscured by dust from new-formed worlds,
> To emblazon the brow of "monkey, langur"
> Give tongue and speech to tree and stone
>
> Who lives and does not know of them
> Eternal the light that is shed by their names
> In the blaze of the sun or deep in her shadow
> So we who come after shall never forget
> That from the dawn of time unto its end
> We are the children of the *Hynñiew Trep*
>
> To you I give thanks, O Land of Mine
> Land where silver rivers flow
> Land where blooms the *Amirphor*
> Whose vivid tones can never fade
> Golden Flower from within whose depths
> The heart receives and overflows

Multitudes teemed under heaven's high vault
Across the land one tongue was heard
A homeland bound by one belief
Traditional colours displayed with pride
Commemoration observance celebration profound
Incomparable the rituals of our native land

Thus lived all those who have gone before
Whose laws were built on sacred writ
Though constant the threat from tiger and *Thlen*
Undefeated their souls, undiminished their hope.
But today we live in other times
Uncertain the journey of our people, our land

High on the hills, deep in the shade
When alone we walk refreshed becalmed
Tell me why O Land of mine
Why does unease disquiet my heart?
When all around I look to see
Why do I feel the ache of tears?

Our hills were our guardians in the past
Who will keep us from harm in days to come?
A down-coursing river is gathering force
A leaden-cloud mass is brooding ahead
But as it was then so tomorrow can be
If again for our homeland together we band

Breathe through us, O wind that blows
Once more that longing "to live for our land"
So once again the heavens will clear
And once again the stars we'll see
The Star of Night becomes the Star of Light
And the Moon once more will rise for us

We share the same sun, same water and wind
In what way then are we different from others?
Sorrow, grief, laughter, joy
It is the same language we all speak
And as we toil to reach the summit
Those down below are human too

From furrows of paddy and beds of millet
A meal we'll provide for the destitute *Phreit*
In numbers we'll grow, become a discernible throng
With Justice and Truth enshrined in our midst
The sky will brighten to a peerless blue
Heralding the coming of a Golden Age

The Peacock will dance when the Sun returns[1]
And she will bathe in the Rupatylli[2]
O Rivers Rilang, Umiam and Kupli[3]
Sweet songs in you will move inspire
Land of Nine Roads, pathways of promise[4]
Where the Mole will strum, the Owl will dance[5]

In the *Asorphi* now forgotten gone[6]
Fires survive continue to burn
For the sake of our beloved *Ri Khasi Ri Pnar*[7]
O Lord to whom this world belongs
Together we'll plough, thresh and build
Ascend from thatch to soaring peaks

---

1   A Khasi tale explaining the eyes on the tail of the Peacock who once upon a time
     lived in the sky with his wife the Sun. But one day as he looked down on the earth
     below he saw a golden-haired maiden with whom he instantly fell in love. He flew
     down only to discover that he had been captivated by a field of golden mustard.
     The foolish peacock was left heartbroken and realised he was doomed to live on
     earth forever. From that time onwards each morning the peacock danced at sunrise
     to greet his wife whose tears would fall on his outspread tail and became the eyes
     on the peacock's tail.
2   The Surma, now in Bangladesh. Here it is compared to a necklace of solid silver.
3   Rivers in the Khasi and Jaiñtia Hills.
4   The Khasi word "*lad*" means both path, or road, as well as opportunity. As
     translating the phrase "*Khyndai lad*" as "Nine Roads" would not reflect the latter
     I added "pathways of promise" in order to better convey the full meaning of the
     original word.
5   Both the Mole and the Owl participate in a dance described in the legend of the
     Sacred Cave where the Sun hid her light to punish living creatures for casting
     doubt on her relationship with her brother the Moon.
6   Precious, treasured, related to the Persian word *Asharfi*, a gold coin issued by
     Persian Kings and the Mughals.
7   "*Ri*" here means land or homeland so "*Ri Khasi Ri Pnar*" means the land or
     homeland of the Khasis and the *Pnar*. Interestingly "*ri*" also means to take care, to
     tend carefully, to preserve.

From brink of waterfalls to verge of deep pools
In a place unknown I find myself
O Lum Shillong, Kyllang, Symper[8]
From you O Land could I ever take flight?
And when I reach the House of God
Of them I will ask—*hangno i Mei?*[9]

 Listen to an audio recording of the poem at
https://doi.org/10.11647/OBP.0137.25

---

8   Shillong Peak. *Kyllang* and *Symper*, see p. 47, n. 11.
9   Where is [my] mother (*i Mei*)? Though the poet does not use the pronoun "my", the honorific "*i*" before "*Mei*" (Mother) immediately indicates to the Khasi reader that the speaker is referring to his mother (as explained at the beginning of this section, the use of "*i*" before "*Mei*" conveys the reverential love Khasi daughters and sons feel for their mother).

Bibliography

Deakin, Roger, *Wildwood: A Journey through Trees* (London: Penguin Books, 2008).

Dkhar, Alvareen, *Na U Kpa Sha U Khun* (Shillong: Shandora Press, self-published, 2013).

May, Andrew, *Welsh Missionaries and British Imperialism: The Empire of Clouds in North-east India* (Manchester and New York: Manchester University Press, 2012).

Nongkynrih, Kynpham Singh, *Around the Hearth, Khasi Legends* (Gurgaon, India: Penguin Books, 2007).

Pugh, F. M., *Ka Jingiarap Ia Ki Kot B. A. Khasi* [*Study Guide for B. A. Khasi Texts*] (Shillong: Shillong Printing Works, 1963).

Rao, Satyajit, *Wild Orchids of Meghalaya — A Pictorial Guide* (Shillong: Meghalaya Biodiversity Board, 2015).

Sawian, Bijoya, *Khasi Myths, Legends and Folk Tales* (Shillong: Ri Khasi Press, 2006).

Sawian, Bijoya, *et al.*, *The Main Ceremonies of the Khasi* (Guwahati: Vivekenanda Kendra Institute of Culture, 2012).

Sten, H. W., *Na Ka Hyndai Sha Ka Lawei* (Shillong: Gratus Publication, 2011).

Tham, Minette, *I Mabah Soso Tham* [*My Uncle Soso Tham*] (Shillong: Shandora Press 1990).

Tham, Soso, *Ki Sngi Barim U Hynñiew Trep* [*The Old Days of the Khasis*] (Shillong: Shillong Printing Works, 1936).

Tham, Soso, *Ki Sngi Barim U Hynñiew Trep*, 3rd ed. (Shillong: Primrose Gatphoh, 1976).

Tham, Soso, *Ka Duitara Ksiar ne ki Poetry Khasi* [*The Golden Duitara, or Khasi Poems*], 8th ed., rev. and enl. (Shillong: Primrose Gatphoh, 1972).

Tham, Soso, *Ka Jingim U Trai Jong Ngi* [a translation of Charles Dickens's *The Life of our Lord*], 2nd ed. ([n.p.], 1936) https://archive.org/details/in.ernet.dli.2015.464546

This is an unglued ebook!

The publication of this book has been made possible through the **Unglue.it** website by contributions from readers like you.

Supporters of this edition:

Ruth & Mark Ellul

ghbonello

randy

Caroline Warman

Benefactors of this edition:

beverly.bevis

Mark Turin

Bibliophiles of this edition:

Jessica E. Smith & Kevin R. Brine Charitable Fund

wendysavage

Gabriella Page-Fort

You can say thank you by supporting the ungluing of more books at **https://unglue.it**

This book need not end here…

At Open Book Publishers, we are changing the nature of the traditional academic book. The title you have just read will not be left on a library shelf, but will be accessed online by hundreds of readers each month across the globe. OBP publishes only the best academic work: each title passes through a rigorous peer-review process. We make all our books free to read online so that students, researchers and members of the public who can't afford a printed edition will have access to the same ideas. This book and additional content is available at:
https://www.openbookpublishers.com/product/746

Customise

Personalise your copy of this book or design new books using OBP and third-party material. Take chapters or whole books from our published list and make a special edition, a new anthology or an illuminating coursepack. Each customised edition will be produced as a paperback and a downloadable PDF. Find out more at:
https://www.openbookpublishers.com/section/59/1

Donate

If you enjoyed this book, and feel that research like this should be available to all readers, regardless of their income, please think about donating to us. We do not operate for profit and all donations, as with all other revenue we generate, will be used to finance new Open Access publications:
https://www.openbookpublishers.com/section/13/1/support-us

Like Open Book Publishers f

Follow @OpenBookPublish 🐦

Read more at the Open Book Publishers **BLOG**

You may also be interested in:

Tellings and Texts
Music, Literature and Performance in North India
Edited by Francesca Orsini and Katherine Butler Schofield

https://www.openbookpublishers.com/product/311

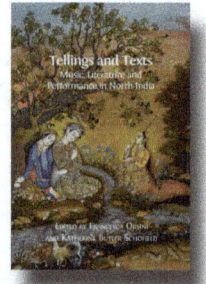

Feeding the City
Work and Food Culture of the Mumbai Dabbawalas
Sara Roncaglia

https://www.openbookpublishers.com/product/87

Oral Literature in the Digital Age
Archiving Orality and Connecting with Communities
Edited by Mark Turin, Claire Wheeler and Eleanor Wilkinson

https://www.openbookpublishers.com/product/186